The God of the Psalms

A Study on the Attributes, Character, and Actions of God in the Psalms

C.A. Wolcott

Formatted and edited by Katie Erickson

ISBN: 9798544721642

Table of Contents

Introduction

This devotional book is a study on the attributes, character, and actions of God as found in the Psalms. One thing I have found very lacking in devotionals is a study on who God is. When I heard Paul Washer ask in a sermon, "When was the last time you heard a sermon on the attributes of God?" that stuck with me. So, I began to include studies of who God is in my own studies and in talks I have given. How can we really understand the Gospel or what our faith is really about if we do not know who God is? That is much of what drove this study.

I started out simply by listing God's attributes as I came across them reading through the Psalms, and I added references to each attribute as found them. For some attributes, I only came across one reference; but for others, I found 20-50 references. In the revision process, I found all the extra references were just a distraction, so I chose instead to cite just one verse which best illustrated the attribute.

I tend to carry an apologetic tone to my writing and in my speaking, so some of the chapters here will include that. It is my desire that this devotional would be a glorification of God and not a mere study of what we can do and learn how to apply it.

Though this is far from comprehensive, I ended up with 90 attributes of God in this study. I want to emphasize here that all 90 of these attributes are true and fully expressed by God all at the same time; we should understand them holistically. There is no contradiction in Him, so God's love, wrath, justice, righteousness, mercy, grace, hatred towards sin, etc. all are 100% true about Him at all times. He does not put one attribute aside to favor another at any time.

I have personally enjoyed doing this study and putting all the different aspects and attributes of God together. May this study be a blessing to you, and I pray as you read and meditate on this book, you pray and meditate on the God we worship for who He really is.

C.A. Wolcott

Chapter 1: Ancient, From of Old

"For God is my King from of old,
Working salvation in the midst of the earth."
~Psalm 74:12

Trees have long been used as markers of history. Many were there before people arrived, and they endure through generations and storms. They are used as landmarks and for events. Lovers carve their initials into a "Kissing Tree." They provide shade, food, and homes for numerous animals. There is a particular kind of tree called a "terabinth" in the Bible, which is a giant, ancient, even "everlasting" tree. The Israelites often deemed these trees to have been around since creation because they were there and well-established long before they arrived. David fought Goliath in the Valley of Elah, the Valley of the Great Tree. He was likely very familiar with this tree during his time as a shepherd, and he knew well the Creator of this tree.

God is the Ancient One. He is from of old and everlasting. He precedes time itself. He is the image of stability and dependability. He does not change according to the winds of the culture which frequently change. When man tries to change the rules, God remains there as a constant reminder and definitive line which cannot be crossed without consequences. God established the rules and the boundaries when He created the universe. While He may suspend or override the physical laws to perform a miracle at times, the physical, logical, and moral laws have never changed. God is not a man that He should lie (Numbers 23:19), nor does He change how He thinks. God always acts in accordance to His character, which stood before the dawn of time.

Like an ancient tree, God demonstrates His strength and His endurance. He provides shelter, food, and shade. He is the ancient one. The people in the past could come to God for the same reason we do today. The way the saints of yesteryear depended upon God and did the impossible is the same way we can depend upon Him today. He does not change, He does not move, and He does not get old. He was there when He made the heavens and the earth. He is before time even began. From before the beginning of time, through Biblical history, He has never changed. Throughout church history He has never changed. He is never out of date either. He is just as relevant and still doing today what He has always done.

What ancient symbol do you turn to for comfort, shelter, and direction? What do you use to get your bearings and location where you are? God is an ever-present shelter in times of storms and attacks. He is the sustenance of our daily lives. He is the anchor of our soul, giving us our place and direction. He is our comfort, giving us shade and rest. He is our historic marker, the place to return to when we have lost our way. He is the Ancient of Days. Turn to Him whenever you have lost your way.

Chapter 2: Avenger

"It is God who avenges me,
And subdues the peoples under me;"
~Psalm 18:47

When the infamous girls' gymnast trainer Larry Nasser was sentenced for molesting a number of the girls under his care, the father of one of the victims charged him at the courthouse. He was tackled by security and the officer who held him down said, "I understand." The father had a rightful rage against the trainer; however, it was not his responsibility to see justice carried out. He rightfully let the courts do their job. But in many cases, the criminal either gets off on a technicality or is never brought to justice by the governmental system. All around the world, corrupt politicians get away with all sorts of heinous crimes, yet every victim is crying out for justice. There is one who is keeping track of every little bit of it: The Avenger.

As a young man, David could practically do no wrong. He conducted himself with such moral character and leadership that after he slew Goliath, the whole nation of Israel was turning to his leadership. But the reigning king, Saul, knew his kingdom would be taken away from him and given to another man, so David became a threat to him. He tried to assassinate David at least 21 recorded times in 1 Samuel. Yet in two of those instances, David had the opportunity to get revenge. In 1 Samuel 24 and 26, Saul was in his hands and he could have easily struck down his enemy. Yet, in both cases, David refused to kill him. He would not take revenge, even though he was the rightfully anointed king. He knew God would avenge him. This attitude is repeated throughout the Psalms.

God is going to avenge every sin committed against a person – if not in that person's lifetime, then certainly on Judgment Day. He asks each of us to forgive our offenders, not because we are to let them off the hook, but to give control of seeing justice done into the hands of God. God longs that each person repents and is born again so they do not have to face His wrath (see 2 Peter 3:9). When God takes His revenge, it is thorough and complete. Some imagine God doing all He can to restrain His anger let it consume us all. That restraint has limits, and Revelation 16 describes how God is going to pour His wrath upon this earth with the bowl Judgments.

It is dangerous to hold anger and bitterness against someone who has wronged you because it will only harm you. Let it go and let God be your Avenger. We do not have the right to take the law into our own hands in our court systems. Neither do we have the right to do so in the spiritual level either. We must take up our case before the Judge to see the wrong made right and let the Judge execute justice as the Law demands. When someone wrongs you, take your case before the Judge of all things. Will He not do what is right?

But what if you are the offender? Turn yourself in to the Judge and He may grant you mercy, lest He avenge the one you have wronged. Take His terms of peace and follow through with how He asks you to carry out your sentence. He will always tell you what you need to do to make things right. He will avenge all sin. Do what you need to do with God lest you be in His path when He comes.

Chapter 3:
Awesome

"He has sent redemption to His people;
He has commanded His covenant forever:
Holy and awesome is His name."
~Psalm 111:9

There are many things in nature which strike us in awe. Mountains, canyons, elk, even some storms like tornadoes tend to draw our attention and make us stare. We look at the Olympians or professional athletes and the marvelous things they are able to do with their physical bodies, and we follow them in wonder. Sometimes we reflect upon our own experiences and revel in how awesome that good experience was.

Yet often, the luster fades. The one who sees the majesty of the Colorado Rockies for the first time, looking at the Back Range tower at 12-14 thousand feet in elevation behind the Front Range which are only at 8 thousand feet, can just stare in amazement, while the one who has lived there his/her whole life can sleep through mountain trips. The star athlete gets injured or gets old and the spotlight fades. Our own highs feel like they are missing something and the glory fades.

The God of the Bible, however, cannot get boring because it is impossible to tap into the depths of how awesome He is. The closer you get to God, the deeper and richer the knowledge of Him becomes. He is not a weak or puny God. He is not limited to physical restraints or time. He is infinite and inexhaustible. When Paul writes about the greatness of God in his letters, he seems to ramble on and on because he simply does not have the language or the words to accurately describe who He is.

God often refused to give His name to man because His name is so great and holy and awesome that man in his finite and sin-cursed mind cannot comprehend it. He told Moses He was the "I AM that I AM." God is everything that any person would ever need. He is our "All in All." His greatness, His majesty, and His glory simply cannot be compared, and yet too often we taken Him for granted. The new, born-again Christian is in a state of constant awe of God, and yet typically after a few years, that awe begins to fade into normalcy. We must constantly be filled with the Holy Spirit because we leak. We get complacent with the awe of God because we get to a point where we think we know all there is to know about Him. Yet the depth we can reach in our knowledge of God is inexhaustible.

The things of this world are going to fade, but the glory of God will never fade. One day we will see the Father face-to-face, and we will then wonder why we never took Him as seriously as we should have. Does being in the presence of God give you awe? Does watching God work make you drop your jaw and stare? Or do you find Him to be boring and unattractive?

God is boring to the sin-filled person who loves his sin more than he loves God. If that describes you, examine yourself and see if you are indeed in the faith. Let God never get boring for us because He is awesome. Take all the thoughts about God written by the saints through all the ages and combined and it will still only scratch the surface of who He is and what He is like. He is an awesome God.

Chapter 4: Beautiful

"One thing I have desired of the Lord,
That will I seek:
That I may dwell in the house of the Lord
All the days of my life,
To behold the beauty of the Lord,
And to inquire in His temple."
~Psalm 27:4

God is beautiful. Beauty is how we describe the pleasure upon the view of a person or object. There is the saying, "Beauty is in the eye of the beholder." There is a lot of truth to that. Some women find certain jewelry beautiful, and others do not. Some men find tools or vehicles beautiful, and others do not. One man's trash is another man's treasure.

David described God as beautiful. David never saw God in person other than perhaps an occasional glance of the Angel of the Lord. However, he had a deep, personal relationship with God and despite his character flaws, he sought after God's heart with everything he had. He knew who God was and what He was like, and he considered that to be beautiful.

There are many who do not consider God to be beautiful. They see him as ugly, distasteful, and everything about Him is not pleasurable. How did David see God as beautiful, but these other people see Him as ugly? The difference is ultimately between those who are born again and those who are not. Those who are born of God see God as beautiful, because they are born of God. Those who are born of sin want nothing to do with God. Self is at natural rebellion and enmity towards God, and that will make Him appear ugly.

Sin changes the appearance of everything and masks it in a false image. It makes that which is evil and against God appear good and pleasing. When the serpent tempted Eve in the Garden of Eden, the fruit became desirable to the eye. First John 2:17-19 warns us about the lust of eyes. That which the sinful flesh calls beautiful will appear that way at first, but the luster quickly fades and then the flesh demands more and more, growing darker and darker. The end leads to death; at this point, nothing is beautiful anymore and the person stays in the darkness because that is all they know.

The born-again believer, however, sees God and the things of God as beautiful. The Christian will see sin and the world's system as ugly because he knows the beauty if offers is fake. It is a pretend beauty. The things of God are everlasting. The beauty of God never wears off to the believer, and all he seeks is more and more of that beauty. That sounds like a drug addict needing stronger and stronger drugs to keep his satisfaction going, but here is the difference. The drug addict needs the stronger drugs because the pleasure he gets from them becomes weaker and weaker. The Christian seeks more and more of God because the pleasure gets better and purer. God is beautiful, and once our eyes catch what He is truly like, they will not be able to pull away.

Chapter 5:
Chooses Us

"For the Lord has chosen Jacob for Himself,
Israel for His special treasure."
~Psalm 135:4

Choosing teams for a pick-up game of any sport is usually a two-sided affair. The captains are usually the two best in the group, and then they pick and choose which ones they believe will best help them win the game. For those who have talent, it feels great to be picked, but there are many eager players who truly don't have a lot of skills, and the others know it. They are usually picked last and only out of obligation, not because of desire. Many of us can related to being on one side or the other, and peer-pressures can make being picked last a miserable experience.

This world picks who they think is the best and looks for the talent to take them to the top. Employers examine the credentials, resumes, and interview appearances and take who they think looks the part. Even the prophet Samuel fell into this mindset when he visited Jesse to anoint a new king in 1 Samuel 16. God told him that He saw something more important: the heart.

God's choices tend to the be the opposite of everyone else's. While the world looks for the best, God looks for the weak, yet the willing. He chooses the weak things to shame the strong, the foolish things to shame the wise, the ignorant to shame the educated, and the poor to shame the rich. He looks for those who know and recognize they can truly do nothing apart from God and actually depend upon Him to do the tasks they need to do. God does not call those who have the skills to do the job; He gives the skills to those He needs to do the job. He looks at the heart and mind of those He created and places them where He needs them to be placed. While they often do not look the part at first, when God takes over and works through them, they are precisely who was needed for that job.

Man in his nature will never choose God. His sinful heart is in defiance and always resistant to God and His ways. Yet, while we were sinners, Christ still died for us (Romans 5:8). We are able to love Him and love others because He first loved us (1 John 4:19). God chooses us and offers us salvation; however, it is up to us to receive it when He offers it. God is under no obligation to choose us, especially in our sin. Yet in His grace and mercy, He does anyway. What an honor and privilege to be chosen by God! Will we take advantage of it?

God chooses the weak and the lowly, and He desires that we do the same thing. Do we care about those whom our society has cast out? The homeless, the orphan, the elderly? What about those in the projects, living on government housing and funding, yet stuck in perpetual poverty with no hope of escape? God has chosen them and sends us to go to them. What about the "black sheep" in the family? It is often the ones that God has chosen who are the ones targeted by the enemy to ensnare in sin so they cannot be used. Do we cast them out too because they got caught? Or should we see them with the potential that God sees them should He get a hold of their lives? Let us choose what God chooses and reject only that which He rejects.

Chapter 6:
Clothes Us

"I will also clothe her priests with salvation,
And her saints shall shout aloud for joy."
~Psalm 132:16

For any rising athlete, very little gives him/her as much pleasure as receiving their earned team jersey with their name on it. Some basketball coaches will not let a player join the team until they have on record to have made one thousand free-throws. Yet when they are handed that jersey, it reveals the coach recognizes them and that they belong to the team. In the military, especially in the old days when army would clash against army, for each soldier to wear the colors of the nation, king, or lord they fought for was critical. That is what determined who was on which side.

There is clothing in the spiritual realm too. When Adam and Eve first lived in the Garden, they were naked and unashamed about it. They did not even know they were naked, and they had nothing to hide. Yet when they sinned, they were exposed, and shame came with it. God told them the day they ate of that tree that they would die, yet for some reason they did not die. Did God lie? No. Someone else died in their place. An animal died so its skins could be used as clothes to cover Adam and Eve and their sin from God's sight. This is the first image of the Gospel. As an animal died to give clothes for Adam and Eve, thus establishing the "doctrine of clothing" which we all adhere to, so Christ died to give "clothes" for all who put their faith and trust in him.

Adam and Eve initially tried to clothe themselves using fig leaves. In the same way, each of us have tried to clothe ourselves with our own righteousness - our own good deeds, our acts of charity, our kindness to others, etc. Yet before the perfect, righteous, and holy God, all those good deeds are nothing more than filthy rags (Isaiah 64:6). It is not because the deeds are faulty, but because the bad deeds, the sin, have corrupted and stained the clothes. Sin is something much more than a sickness to be cured. It is a curse which must be broken. The only thing able to undo the curse is death. And yet in the great scandal of grace, Jesus willingly paid that unpayable debt and died in our place so that we might live. He offers His Blood, His life, and His sustenance to cover our sin so when God looks at us, He does not see a sin-covered, vile human, He sees His own righteous Son.

What clothes are you wearing? Does your jersey show that you play for God's Kingdom or for yourself? Are you wearing what the world wants to see, or are you standing firm, taking a stand that says, "I am on God's team"? To wear God's clothes means you are an opponent to self and an opponent to this world. You cannot wear your own righteousness or worldly wisdom and then claim to be on God's side. You must forsake those clothes, strip naked before God (not literally), and ask for His clothes. Only then will we be properly clothed. The clothes of the sinful self and of the world will be exposed and stripped away from them. It is always best to do it before God on His terms before it's too late. God offers them for free, but only for a limited time. Take advantage of the offer.

Chapter 7: Comforter

"Show me a sign for good,
That those who hate me may see it and be ashamed,
Because You, Lord, have helped me and comforted me."
~Psalm 86:17

David called for God to present a sign not for him but for those who hate him to see it and see that God was indeed on his side. He had already received help from the Lord before, and he took comfort in that help. But here, David wanted conformation to show to his enemies that God had already acted on his behalf.

God comforts his people. He will avenge those who harm His children. He will bring rest and restitution to those who are His. When the enemy steals from His people, God will restore four times that which was stolen. That does not give anyone liberty to sin nor to blow off resources. But it does give comfort that nothing can be taken by force which will not be restored.

God is not a fluffy comforter. He is not the stereotypical mother who pats her child on the head as he cries saying, "It's okay." He wants His children to cry on His shoulder, but He also grieves with them and is going to do something about it. Maybe not right away, maybe not in the "preferred" timing or manner, but He will do something about it. There is no sin which will go unpunished, and He especially will not allow sins against His children go unpunished.

God's solutions are not platitudes. God is never going to give a simple pat-on-the-back answer that tells just what the person wants to hear. He will say what needs to be heard. A true answer, even when it brings judgment, will always be a greater comforter than a lie intended to do nothing more than appeal to emotions. Little illustrates this better than Pharaoh, Nebuchadnezzar, and Belshazzar when dreams and visions took place.

In Genesis 41, Pharaoh had the dream of a coming great harvest and a terrible famine afterwards. It greatly troubled him, and none of his wise men could provide an answer which comforted him. Joseph did. Daniel did the same with Nebuchadnezzar's dream in Daniel 2. The king was so troubled by the dream and knew his own wise men were just trying to buy time to give him an answer he wanted to hear. Only Daniel could provide comfort. Daniel 5 has an even more interesting case because Belshazzar saw the writing on the wall, and after Daniel interpreted the writing and foretold of his own doom, Belshazzar promoted Daniel to number three in the kingdom. Why? Because he heard the truth and it comforted him.

God is a comforter of his people. He will speak truth in all cases, and truth will always give more peace and relief than any 'feel-good' lie. No troubles will go unanswered, and all of God's people can take comfort in that.

Chapter 8:
Compassion

"But You, O Lord, are a God full of compassion, and gracious, Longsuffering and abundant in mercy and truth."
~Psalm 86:15

God is compassionate. He understands what each person is going through and the circumstances which have influenced each decision made. He also sees the motives behind each decision. When Jesus looked upon the crowds during His ministry, He saw them as sheep without a shepherd. The people were helpless, lost, confused, following whoever moved in whatever direction, and easily subdued by the wolves of their day. Empathy is an emotion we experience when we see someone hurting. Compassion is a choice to do something about it. Jesus never stopped with empathy. He has compassion upon these people.

But Jesus was not a pushover. He had compassion when He saw the crowds before feeding the 5000. However, John 6 details this feeding, the walking on water miracle, and then the addressing of the crowed who wanted more food. The people noticed that Jesus had no feast prepared for them yet managed to feed everyone, and they wanted to see Him put on another show. The second time, Jesus did not have the same compassion. He saw their hearts and knew they did not want truth, just more food. His message about not seeking physical food but instead seeking His flesh and His blood, that their sustenance would be Him, was so hard that it is estimated that 20,000 people left Him and ceased following Him. Jesus then turned to His disciples and asked if they wanted to go, too.

Jesus was compassionate but not gullible. He would not allow people to play the victim with Him nor appeal to emotions to manipulate Him. He responded to genuine and raw emotion, the desperation of knowing He was the only hope they had. Jesus frequently moved to address the physical needs initially, but He always went from physical need to spiritual need.

In the Parable of the Sheep and Goats (Matthew 25), Jesus showed how the sheep would tend to the physical needs of the lost, but the goats would not. A Christian who reflects Christ is someone who will tend to the poor and the destitute but will also be wise enough to know against being played the fool. As God showed us compassion in our sufferings, let us in return show compassion to those around us who are suffering.

Chapter 9: Conquers Enemies

"Through God we will do valiantly,
For it is He who shall tread down our enemies."
~Psalm 108:13

In nearly all the great action movies, there is a moment where the hero leads the final charge against the enemy forces, faces off with the villain, and walks away the victor. Luke Skywalker charges down the Death Star trench with Darth Vader on his heels. Aragorn rallies the Men of the West in a final stand against Sauron's forces at the Black Gate of Mordor. Hector and Achilles raise the moral of Troy and Greece respectively. Iron Man and Captain America lead the charge against Thanos. Their leadership gives their armies strength and courage to do the impossible.

Many real battles were won not merely because of the courage of soldiers and the strength of the leadership, but because of the prayers of the saints. Rees Howells ran a Bible college during World War II and turned the college into a war room. He had maps of where soldiers were, with a radio constantly giving updates on the war. He led his college into prayer for the soldiers with the mindset that they were on the front lines, where life or death were the only options. On the European front, the Germans kept outpowering and outgunning the Allies and yet the Allies kept winning. The only explanation was the hand of God moving on behalf of the praying saints.

God is not a pacifist, a being only about love and grace and mercy. While He is all those things, He is also a warrior who will conquer and defeat His enemies. Ever since Satan rebelled against God, he has been waging war ever since, trying to gather as many forces as he can, both spiritual and physical. He tricked Eve into eating the fruit of the Tree of the Knowledge of Good and Evil, and Adam did nothing but take part of the deed. The sinful nature is by definition at war with God, and God is going to defeat sin, death, and the devil once for all one day. He tarries and waits because He longs to save man from that day of conquest. He sends us as ambassadors to call for peace before God comes with His army where He will singlehandedly destroy all that which wages war against Him.

In the meantime, God has given us equipment to engage in this battle, to stand our ground, and fight with God as our Commander-in-Chief. The Armor of God of Ephesians 6:10-18 is not a child's toy but real armor for a real battle on a real battlefield and against a real enemy. This enemy is not flesh and blood, people seduced or coerced into the war against God, but against their puppeteers, the forces of darkness, the authorities and the philosophies enslaving people.

There is no neutral side in this war. We are either for God or against Him, but we can't be neutral. He forces each person to make a choice, and delaying the choice is no different than saying "no." God will conquer His enemies and as long as we continue to live in our sin, not taking His offers and terms of peace, we will remain His enemies. Accept His terms of peace. The world will turn against you, but they are on the losing side. That is not where you want to be. Jesus will return at the Conquering King and in that day, all that is wrong will be made right.

Chapter 10: Considers Man

"What is man that You are mindful of him,
And the son of man that You visit him?"
~Psalm 8:4

Many skeptics say, "If this whole universe is just a home for man, it seems like a waste of space." In a way they are right. If all the vastness of space, the stars, the galaxies, and everything exists solely for just man to exist on planet Earth, then what is the point of having all this extra stuff out there? But is the purpose of this universe just to provide a home for mankind? The answer is no. This whole universe is a display the grandeur and glory of God.

Some of the stars of this universe are so big they would swallow the bulk of our solar system. Betelgeuse is twice the diameter of earth's orbit around the sun, and Canis Majoris is bigger than Saturn's orbit. Galaxies slated to measure 100,000 light years across and a universe expanding beyond measure make this earth appear very small. In fact, when the Voyager probe passed Neptune, it turned around to take snapshots of the journey back and one picture was the famed "Pale Blue Dot," a shot of the earth captured in a beam of light. And yet, God cares about each of the seven billion people (and counting) on this earth.

Who is man that God would be mindful of him? Why should God care about each individual? He has all this huge universe to run and the life of each person is little more than a vapor. Yet He is interested and involved in even the little things of each person. Genesis makes clear that the stars and planets and galaxies are not the crowning jewel of God's creation. The stars, as massive and majestic as they are, were given a little footnote after the sun and moon were created. The crowning moment was man. There is nothing in creation which compares to man. How?

Nothing else in creation was made in the image of God nor given moral responsibility of actions. No animal is held responsible for how it acts, but every person is. God takes interest even in small things. He made a borrowed axe head float in 2 Kings 6. He sent Elijah to a widow in a Gentile town during the 3 ½ year drought in 1 Kings 17. He focused His attention towards the weak, the poor, the destitute, those whom society had left behind.

God directed all these massive objects for man's benefit. All the stars are placed not merely to give God glory but to give man signs for the times, navigational skills, and seasonal indicators. Astronomers have found that from any other place in the universe, all the stars would actually point towards earth, rather than make their own constellations. The universe was made for both man and for God's glory. Man is small and insignificant compared to the universe but uniquely made in the image of God.

Who is man that God should consider him? That is a question every person should be asking in humility, knowing that God is mightier than everything else. Yet He is concerned for each and every one. Yes, that includes both you and me.

Chapter 11:
Cornerstone

"The stone which the builders rejected
Has become the chief cornerstone."
~Psalm 118:22

A building is only as strong as its foundation. The Leaning Tower of Pisa in Italy leans because the ground it was built upon sank. In San Francisco, the Millennium Building is leaning to the point where it is uninhabitable and also cannot be brought down due to the surrounding buildings. Yet there are churches, roads, and other buildings in Europe which have lasted centuries to millennia through storms and earthquakes. How? They had a firm foundation which did not shake nor move when the disaster struck.

A cornerstone is the anchoring rock to build a building. The entire foundation is determined by this stone as well as the size, strength, and dimensions of the building. The larger and stronger the stone, the taller and bigger the building can be. But if the stone is weak, brittle, or does not provide an anchor for any other foundation stones, then for the building to survive, it must be small and short, and even then, there is no promise of it surviving a storm.

The chief cornerstone for Christianity is Christ. It is not doctrines of faith (though those are very important), nor church traditions, nor proclamations, nor good deeds, but Christ, the second person of the Trinity. Paul told the Corinthian church he did not come with a well-crafted, eloquent, emotion-stirring speech, but a demonstration of the power of the Holy Spirit in his life. Paul was the scholar among scholars of his time, and yet he chose that all his knowledge was worth nothing next to knowing Christ and the work of the cross. Paul did not merely claim that Christ was his cornerstone, but he lived it.

What is the foundation of our faith? Many people only believe Christianity because they were raised that way. Others found a speaker or preacher they liked, and their entire doctrines and way of thinking come exclusively from that preacher or set of preachers. Many Christians have a "pet doctrine" that they elevate over others. Some are dependent upon "evidence" and will quickly change positions if the "evidence" starts to point another direction. Others want to mix and match their foundations, thinking it is perfectly fine to believe in the secular accounts of humanism in regards to origins and in Jesus Christ at the same time. The problem with each of these positions is that Christ is not the cornerstone, let alone the chief cornerstone. In any of these positions, Christ is at most relegated to decorations on the walls.

Christianity is built upon Christ. All the sermons, all the doctrines, all the science, all of it must match and agree with Christ or it does not belong. If you are stuck in any of these areas, the easiest answer is to strip down your entire library of resources to nothing. Start with a single volume which is Christ, and then start rebuilding your library from there (I give credit to Eric Ludy and his sermon, "Christophany" for this.) Is Christ the center and the foundation for your life? Or do you even give Him the privilege of playing second fiddle? Christ only has one place of honor: front and center stage and He will not share it. That is where He belongs. Let us build with Him there.

Chapter 12: Counselor

"I will bless the Lord who has given me counsel;
My heart also instructs me in the night seasons."
~Psalm 16:7

It is always wise to get counsel before making a big decision. Schools hire a group of counselors to help students with scheduling their classes and preparing for college but also dealing with the myriad of in-school situations. Large companies hire counselors for their employees. People turn to financial experts to help with their investments, or a lawyer for criminal or civil cases. Even the President of the United States has a group of counselors who help him make decisions.

There are good counselors and bad counselors, and there are good responses and bad responses to counsel. Moses listened to the counsel of his father-in-law who suggested his set up a system of God-fearing, respectable judges who could handle most of the cases of the large congregation while he took the big cases (Exodus 18). Rehoboam, son of Solomon, rejected his father's counselors and instead turned to his peers who sent him on a power trip. That led to the dissolution of the kingdom into Israel and Judah (1 Kings 12).

There is one counselor above them all: God Almighty. Who better to turn to than the one who knows every detail about every situation? Hezekiah and Jehoshaphat demonstrated this when facing sickness (2 Kings 20) and three armies (2 Chronicles 20). Yet Asa got a foot disease and did not turn to the counsel of the Lord, but instead to the doctors (2 Kings 16). God rebuked him for it, and he died as a result.

God is not against doctors, but He seeks that we turn to Him *first*. He has sent many people to the doctors to deal with cancer not because He cannot heal but so they can be a witness to the medial field (among other reasons).

Where is our first turn? Who do we seek counsel from? If we were honest, most of us use God as a last resort when all else fails. Why not turn to Him first, get what He has to say about the situation, and do what He says about it? The world will always have a counteroffer, and it will often be in direct defiance or opposition to the counsel of God. God's counsel is about His Kingdom first and foremost with the entire picture in mind. The world's counsel is about protecting you and your immediate needs at the expense of others and with no real grip of potential consequences down the road.

Seek God's counsel first in any situation. The more our decisions are led by God, the less we will regret those decisions. They may require a season of pain and suffering but will always be worth it. Facing a job choice? Seek where God wants you to work. Facing a choice of marriage? Ask God to reveal whom He wants you to marry. Facing a financial crisis? Ask God to help you manage your resources and provide for your needs, even if it means cutting down on lifestyle choices. Facing a family crisis? Ask God for wisdom and patience. And in the ultimate case, if it comes down to choosing to deny God or die, let God prepare you for that decision to already be made before it comes. God's counsel is always good, always perfect, and always succeeds. Seek Him first and obey His commands when they come.

Chapter 13:
Covers Sin

"You have forgiven the iniquity of Your people;
You have covered all their sin."
~Psalm 85:2

When a pastor or church leader is exposed in a scandalous affair, be it a marital affair, sexual abuse of children, or financial extortion, the media and the world are quick to jump on the story and make it as public as possible, regardless of if the allegations are true or not. Especially in today's realm of politics, if someone running for office is not liked by the "politically correct" for being clean, they often search for anything possible to discredit them in the eyes of the public, and even sometimes make it up. In some cases, the exposure is deserving because God was trying to deal with an area of sin, they would not repent, and God had to expose it. But that is not His preferred method.

God would rather show mercy and cover sin rather than expose it. There is a difference between covering sin and hiding it or sweeping it under the rug. When one hides someone else's sin that they see, they turn a blind eye. They know it is there, but they simply choose not to deal with it or expose it because they do not want to get involved. Someone covering sin, however, would rather work with that person in private and get the sin out in private rather than expose them to public shame and humiliation.

Little demonstrates this notion more than Jesus dealing with the woman caught in adultery in John 8. She was caught in the very act, and a mob gathered to expose her publicly and to get Jesus on a moral dilemma. He could deny the Law and spare her, or He could be ruthless and defend the Law. Jesus, in effect, said, "Go ahead and stone her, but let the one without this sin cast the first stone." He knew these men likely did not stumble across her but were "peeping toms." Jesus did not accuse her, nor let her accusers do so when they were guilty, too. However, He did not turn a blind eye to her sin either. He told her to, "Go and sin no more." He covered her sin and had the ability to do so because of what He was going to do on the cross.

There were other times where it was appropriate to call out sin. John the Baptist called out Herod for sleeping with his brother's wife. Jesus called out the Pharisees in public for their false teachings. Paul sometimes even cited specific names like "Alexander the coppersmith" for doing him harm. But in all these cases, the motivation was never to "bring them down" but to keep people alert for sin and false teachings. When David tried to cover his adultery with Bathsheba (2 Samuel 11), God told him his son would do the same sin in public (2 Samuel 16:21-22).

God is going to deal with sin one way or the other. If we work with God and confess it, rather than hide it, then God will cover it and not let the public get access to it. There are times and places to expose sin, namely in the events of crimes being done, however, treat the sins against you as God treats your sins against Him. Cover them when God tells you to and only expose them when God tells you to. Do not confuse exposing sin with gossip and slander, because they do look similar. God covered your sin with Christ's blood. Likewise, cover the sins of your brothers.

Chapter 14: Creator, Maker, Builder

*"By the word of the Lord the heavens were made,
And all the host of them by the breath of His mouth."*
~Psalm 33:6

The creative imagination of a child is incredible to behold. They are able to take the simplest of things and come up with all sorts of ideas about what it is or can do. A stick becomes a lightsaber. A mishmash of Legos becomes a spaceship. With a pencil or crayon, a fantasy creature comes alive. One of the greatest tragedies is when that creativity is squashed, because these are the kids who can become inventors and entrepreneurs or are able to discover the one angle or detail that makes an idea suddenly work. Man is meant to be creative, and that creativity is a reflection of where we came from.

God is the Creator. He is the one who made this universe and built it all together. The more we study science, the more we should be in awe of how God put it all together simply by speaking it into existence. Just examine DNA. In recent years, our knowledge of how it works has exploded, and the fingerprints of God are everywhere. This molecule, millions of base-pairs of nucleotides long, makes any computer program look like child's play. DNA can be read forwards and backwards to create a protein. It can read every 5th or so nucleotide to make another. DNA is folded into different 3D shapes, each able to produce yet another set of proteins. In certain circumstances, DNA can be refolded into another shape to produce even more proteins to deal with that situation. It is amazing. Only the mind of an infinite God could produce such a system.

As an author creates the world of his/her book, so God is the author of history and what goes on in this universe. He is telling the greatest epic story of all time, and each of us is a character in that story. Each of us is a major character in our own subplots, which all tie completely cohesively to the main story line, which is God's dealings with mankind. He made the setting, He set the conditions for each character to go through, and He actively plays the role of the Hero of the story. Any good author lets the characters determine what they will do, when, and how, and God does the same with us. But as the Author, He has a goal that He is going to accomplish and will set the conditions for each of us to respond in such a way to get it done. We have the option of going along with Him or fighting against Him.

Since God is our Creator, should we not turn to Him to find out how and why He made us? Each of us are corrupted by sin when we are born; God did not make us that way. He seeks to redeem us FROM that curse and is in process of re-making us into the image of Jesus Christ. Let the Creator finish the job He started. He who is in Christ is a new creature (2 Corinthians 5:17). We are the clay. He is the potter. But woe to the clay which cannot and will not be used. The clay which does the job it was made to do is put to use. Let us be put to use by the Creator.

Chapter 15:
Defender, Guardian, Keeps Watch

"Unless the Lord builds the house,
They labor in vain who build it;
Unless the Lord guards the city,
The watchman stays awake in vain."
~Psalm 127:1

Being a watchman is not an easy job. The Border Patrol agents on the borders of our country have a very difficult job having to be suspicious of every person, knowing the vast majority who come through the border are legitimately good people. The drug cartels and smugglers do everything they can to get their goods across the borders without being caught Often to do so, they have to look like an ordinary citizen to get by suspicion. Sometimes it works, sometimes it doesn't. It is even harder for the Border Patrol when entire border is not secure, and they have to constantly patrol the desert for illegals. Many get through.

The best efforts of man will always fall short in protecting what is important to us. The common thief may be deterred by some protective measures, but if there is something he wants, he will find a way into the most secure vault. Some even take that as a challenge or a dare. Our best efforts have weaknesses, and all it takes is a moment of dropping our guard for the sting to take place.

There is only one guard who can protect us at all times: God. He is the only one who never gets tired or sleeps, He always knows the motive of each person and their intentions, and He sees everything so there is no going behind His back either. If God wants to protect something, it will be protected, and nothing can faze it. The nation of Israel endured assault after assault after assault and yet they always remained. The born-again believer is also protected by God to do the impossible as long as he/she is obedient to God's plan. Read Christian biographies. The things they did were impossible and against all odds, yet because God watched over them, they succeeded. All those who tried to guard themselves always failed to protect themselves.

The church has been entrusted with guarding and protecting the Word of God. One of our jobs is to guard and protect the Bible and the message it contains with absolute dedication and, if necessary, to give our lives to not have it be assaulted or blasphemed. As we do so, God will be our protector and our guardian. He will not let us be touched until it is time. Look at Jesus, John the Baptist, or Paul and how many times they escaped peril. The same God who guarded them is the One who guards us. Unless God is the one who guards us, nothing we do will stand. We don't need to stand for ourselves. Let God defend us. He's better at it than we could be anyway.

Chapter 16: Deliverer, Rescuer

"The Lord is my rock and my fortress and my deliverer;
My God, my strength, in whom I will trust;
My shield and the horn of my salvation, my stronghold."
~Psalm 18:2

There is an interesting observation between the testimonies of those who came out of Christianity and reject it and those who came out of any other belief system into Christianity. The former talk about what led them to leave Christianity and the reason will usually be some form of education or "enlightenment." The latter talk about how they came out of drug use, pornography, atheism, Islam, Hinduism, etc., and the common description of what got them out is in terms of deliverance. They were rescued from what they used to believe or be hooked to. This is not a mere "Christianese" term to describe it, but an actual, real deliverance - a freedom from something they thought was their way of life.

Deliverance is when someone is in trouble and someone else comes in and saves them from that trouble. God determined to judge the world with a massive Flood and instructed Noah to build an ark through which to save himself, his family, and the land-dwelling, air-breathing animals. The ark had plenty of space for other people, but only eight entered. God rescued Jacob and his family by sending Joseph ahead to Egypt to prepare for it. Then when Israel was enslaved by Egypt, God sent Moses to be their deliverer and establish them as their own nation. Shadrach, Meshach, and Abednego believed God would deliver them from the fiery furnace, yet even if He did not, they still would not bow before Nebuchadnezzar's idol.

Jesus arrived not to rescue the Jews from Rome, but to rescue man from sin. Jesus was not interested in merely rescuing us from the penalty of sin, which is eternal torment in Hell. He was sent to rescue us from sin itself, from sin having control over our lives. Jesus did not die to help keep you out of hell (though that is part of the package). He died to save you from *you*. The biggest problem any of us face is not global warming, nor World War III, nor COVID, nor the government taking our liberties. The biggest problem any of us face is ourselves. Jesus came to save us from us.

But this rescue does not come automatically. While it is free for us and cannot be earned, it cost Jesus His life and it will cost us our life as we know it. We must forsake our life of sin to be rescued. Yet many of us find ourselves in a prison cell, with the door unlocked. We not only want to stay in the prison cell in its "comforts," but we think that door will be open for us to leave whenever we want. As long as we stay in the prison cell, we are still prisoners. However, that door does not open whenever we want; it is only open when God opens it. We must take advantage of the offer when it is offered. Every person is guaranteed at least one chance to take this offer, but no one is guaranteed more than one.

God is the Deliverer. He is our Rescuer. If we keep returning back to our sin, are we truly delivered? God came to save us. Let Him save you, and then return the favor by forsaking that which He rescued you from and following Him to where true freedom lies.

Chapter 17:
Directs Steps, Leads, Guides,

"The steps of a good man are ordered by the Lord,
And He delights in his way."
~Psalm 37:23

In 2011, a professional pool trick shot artist and missionary landed in El Paso, Texas, to do a couple shows, except for one problem. El Paso was in the middle of a freeze so bad it shut down the city for a week. Water mains burst and even the power generators froze requiring rolling blackouts. The venues shut down for him. Yet God provided new venues and a totally different audience than expected. To this day, he cites that trip as one of the best events he ever did in his previous 15 years of doing trick shot shows all over the world. This story can be found in Steve Lillis' autobiography, *But You Must.*

If you were to count the number of times you actually were able to carry out your plans as intended, you might be hard pressed to get to your second hand. Our plans fall apart all the time, yet not once is it out of God's control or His plan. Sometimes the plans fall apart because of bad choices we make, or sometimes it is bad choices someone else makes. The general of an army wants every one of his soldiers to do as commanded, and if just one disobeys orders or breaks line too early, it can turn a sure victory into defeat. But there are times where the plans fail because God needs to redirect us.

With the pool trick shot show example above, none of God's redirecting would have happened had the plans not been made, the plane tickets paid, and the events scheduled. God is not capable of re-directing feet which are not moving.

He would have to get people moving first, then He can direct them.

Life is full of detours which often lead to a complete change of direction for the course of life. One of the problems is that we think in terms of the destination and arriving, when often God is concerned about the journey. The only destination we truly need to be concerned about is our ultimate destination: where we will spend eternity. But in this life, God has no plans for us to "settle" in a career or just to "work until retirement." He wants to use us every minute of our lives, no matter how young or old we are. God has no retirement age on this earth, and as long as you are alive and kicking, God is able to put you to use.

Do not be discouraged when your plans change. They never were meant to be carried out. If you had gone through with them, you likely would not like the actual results. Sometimes God changes our plans to protect us, and other times He redirects us to bring us to something even better than we imagined from our original plans. If we are obedient and follow Him, no matter what the cost, we will not regret it. Not a single person who has devoted their lives to following and serving God with all their heart would take it back, even if it meant going through some brutal hardships. Let Him direct and guide you. He's got bigger and better plans than we ever could.

Chapter 18: Endures

"Your name, O Lord, endures forever,
Your fame, O Lord, throughout all generations."
~Psalm 135:13

Fencing is an unusual sport where endurance is more on display than most other sports. Athletes at the top levels practice for hours upon end so that come game time, they can play at full capacity for the duration of the game, which is usually 2-3 hours including all breaks. But the larger fencing tournaments can last 8-10 hours for those who make the finals. At that point, it is not a matter of skill level but endurance.

In 1980, Coach Herb Brooks led the U.S. Men's Hockey Team to upset the USSR team, which was easily the strongest team in the world. In the 2004 movie *Miracle* depicting this moment, Coach Brooks did not want to be the most talented team, but he did promise his team that they would be the most conditioned. During that epic game, no team had ever been able to skate with the Russians through the end of the game. The U.S. team had the endurance to keep pace and withstand the Russian offense.

There is a battle for truth greater than any game or sport. The thing about truth is that truth endures. It is able to withstand the best moves and attacks from the opposition and will remain standing in the end. Satan, the world, all the experts, all the rulers, and all the authorities can gather their full forces with all their arguments "refuting" the Bible, and yet they all pass away while God's name endures.

The French humanist Voltaire is famous for saying, "Within 100 years of my lifetime, the Bible will not be found anywhere except museum displays." He thought that with his arguments, he had completely nullified the Bible's influence from society. Yet 50 years after his death, the Geneva Bible Society bought his house and filled it to the ceiling with Bibles.

The skeptics and the nations rage against God and His Word, and yet they all pass, and the Bible still remains. The Bible has survived 2000 years (and counting) of intense scrutiny, persecution, and rejection even over the tiniest of details, and yet not a single objection has ever been found to hold water. Numerous apologists such as Sir William Ramsay, C. S. Lewis, Josh McDowell, Lee Strobel, and Francis Shaeffer initially sought to disprove the Bible, and yet in their honest investigations all they could do was find proof that it was indeed true. The Bible endures because its Author endures.

Do you fear the scientists and the philosophers who think the Bible is outdated and no longer relevant? Does reading the "latest find" that refutes the Bible make you worry about your faith? Are you going through hardships and are not sure if you are going to make it out in one piece? Do not fear because the very Christ who endured the cross and death lives within you and will not let you fail. No matter what the enemy throws at you, you can endure because He endures. Take shelter in Christ and nothing will touch you.

Chapter 19: Eternal, Everlasting

*"Your kingdom is an everlasting kingdom,
And Your dominion endures throughout all generations."
~Psalm 145:13*

Video games have been around for nearly 40 years and counting. From consoles to portables to PC, the gaming industry is massive today. Yet each generation of consoles only lasts a few years before a new one by the respective company is released. While some consoles last longer, after every ten years or so, it is nearly impossible to find the games or systems outside of vintage stores.

Sports are very similar. The Super Bowl is one of the biggest single events watched by the whole world each year as sports analysts discuss to death every detail about each team and player in the big game. Yet aside from sport fanatics (or those with really good memories) who remembers who won the Super Bowl five or ten years ago, let alone against whom?

There is a big problem with these things: they do not last. The "test of time" is extremely short as there are still people around who remember when the first video game or the first Super Bowl was ever played. Now there is nothing wrong with playing a game or watching a sport in itself, but Jesus warned against storing up treasures here on earth where they can break down, or get stolen, or simply fade into history. Instead, store treasures in heaven which are eternal and will never be lost.

God is the eternal God. He is everlasting, and His kingdom is everlasting. He endures because He is everlasting. Nothing temporal is ever going to faze Him nor His work. While God interacts with us in the here and now, He always has the big picture of eternity in mind. He looks at what things will affect us not just now but also down the road both in the immediate future and in eternity. The thing God treasures the most is our souls. Once we die and we have not been saved through the work of the cross, we will be lost in hell forever. He longs that none of us perish but that all might repent to the saving knowledge of Christ (2 Peter 3:9).

Leonard Ravenhill once lamented that we all need "eternity stamped upon our eyeballs." We need to see everything from the eternal perspective. The crises we are facing now - how will they affect us eternally? Are they a big deal at all, or are they simply to prepare us for something bigger and better? Do we look at other people with eternity in mind? Do we care enough to wonder if they will be going to hell or not? So many of us live in complacency where we are only concerned about ourselves here and now. Let us instead live with eternity in our eyes.

What can you do that will have everlasting influences? Sometimes the smallest act of kindness can be all that is needed to change a life. God is interested in you being available, not your talents. Let him use you for eternal values. Ray Boltz's song "Thank You" describes how little things can lead to a great reward in heaven: lives who would not be there otherwise. You cannot change or save the world, but you can save some around you, if you let God use you for it. Think eternally and how what you do will affect someone's eternal destination.

Chapter 20: Exalted

"For You, Lord, are most high above all the earth;
You are exalted far above all gods."
Psalm 97:9

Graduation day is a day of celebration and honor for completing a set of courses in education. It is a time to give praise and recognition to the graduate. Upon winning a championship, the winning team gets a parade through their home city and often an invite to the White House to meet the president. Many cultures give titles to distinguished persons, such as Knight, Baron, or Lord. Celebrities always have a paparazzi following them, exalting them into glorified positions.

All the praise of man is for here and now, and it is temporary. The spotlight only lasts for a season, and even then, many of these celebrities in the spotlight are miserable. Receiving the praise of man does not satisfy because it is short-lived. It is not often even sincere because of how quickly it can disappear. In reality, the real praise needs to go somewhere higher and better.

Man is able to accomplish many things that are incredible, yet that ability comes from one source: God himself. Paul took absolutely no accolades for himself. Anything good he did, he attributed to God, but he took ownership of his own sin. He gave God all the praise and exaltation he could offer. God is the only one worthy of all the praise and glory and honor. When God presented a scroll to open in heaven, John moaned that no one was worthy to open it. Then Jesus entered the picture, the Lamb who had been slain (Revelation 5). He was the one worthy to open the scroll.

Jesus came down to earth and took the form of a man, living exactly like any ordinary man, except He was completely and fully yielded to God. While He was fully God by identity, He was also fully man by identity and lived as such. He did not use any "God-powers" to do what He did. He took on the cross, the judgment of God for the sin of man, and bore His full wrath. Yet after dying, three days later, He rose again and now is exalted to the right hand of the Father, the position of highest honor. He is exalted and given the name that is above every name. All authority is given to Him and all the nations is under His rule. He is exalted.

Where is God in our lives? Is He the headliner and the one front and center on the stage? Or is He pushed aside to the back of the stage, if He's even allowed on it? God is to be first and foremost in our lives, and He will not share the spot-light nor play second fiddle. He is either Lord of all in our lives or not Lord at all. Yet no matter where we try place Him in our lives, He still is the supreme ruler over everything and is not subject to our whims.

Let us give God the praise that He deserves. We have no qualms about recognizing a sports team for their championship season, a scientist for a Nobel Prize, or a hero for saving someone's life. Each of them would be insulted to give praise to someone else for doing what they did. Likewise, God is insulted when we exalt someone for what He did instead of exalting God for what He did. He is exalted whether we praise Him or not. Let us give Him that praise.

Chapter 21: Faithfulness

"Your faithfulness endures to all generations;
You established the earth, and it abides."
~Psalm 119:90

Longevity is a rarity in both sports and the workplace today. When a player stays with the same team for a 15- to 20-year career, that player's jersey is often retired, especially if they were a good player. Employers have a difficult time finding employees who last more than 20 years for the same company. Some have the same career but rarely the same company. Sometimes that is not the player or employee's choice, but often times it is. The idea of faithfulness and loyalty is rare to find.

People frequently shift around from church to church as well. If something goes wrong, people leave their church rather than stick around and work the problem out. This attitude is also seen in many family units where "until death do you part" has no meaning. Many couples are no longer making the commitment to marriage and just "live together." These rarely last because there is no faithfulness to the end.

God is a faithful God. He finishes what He set out to do and does what He committed to do. He never backs down on a promise and will see each one through to completion. Sometimes God answers immediately. He told Jehoshaphat that He would march to battle and win without having to raise a sword. The king believed Him, worshipped right then and there, and then when it came time for the battle, he sent out his singers and worshippers as the front line. When he arrived, the three armies had already defeated each other.

In other cases, God acts through generations. Abraham never saw his seed grow to more than two grandsons, yet generations after that, Moses walked out of Egypt with 600,000 men. Both Abraham and David were promised that through their line, the Savior, the King of Kings, would come. Yet around 2000 years after Abraham and 1000 years after David, Jesus arrived. God fulfills each of His promises both for hope and for judgment. Sometimes He will delay a judgment. When Josiah led Judah to a nationwide revival, it did not stop the judgment from his grandfather's sin from coming, but it delayed it to after his death. It still came, through. About 500 of the 2500 prophecies in the Bible remain unfulfilled as they deal with the end times, but the Bible's track record show that they will be fulfilled to the letter.

Why do we doubt God to carry through on what He said? Why is it that so many of us can see God come through with those around us but we don't believe He will do it for us? God is faithful. Did He promise it? If so, He will come through. It is our responsibility to believe and be patient for Him to come through. He will come. Daniel had to wait three weeks for an answer to his vision of the man because of the spiritual battle taking place (Daniel 10). God is faithful with us; let us be faithful to Him. Yet even when we fail, He is faithful still. God started a work in us when He saved us. He will see it through to completion. He is faithful.

Chapter 22: Father

*"A father of the fatherless, a defender of widows,
Is God in His holy habitation."*
~Psalm 68:5

The life of a military child is not easy. After the father is deployed and moved on assignments, the family either is without the father or is constantly on the move, without the opportunity to grow up with the same friends or attend the same schools. But very little captures the love of a father when he arrives home from deployment to surprise his child either in school or whatever event they are in. The military child understands his/her father may not return home or may not return home in one piece.

There are many orphans in this world who lost their father due to sickness, disease, war, murder, incarceration, or abandonment. Then there are many children whose fathers live at home but are never home due to working 80-90 hours a week. Many fathers see their roles as to simply provide for the food, toys, sports, home, cars, etc. Then when they are not doing that, their "manhood" is just partying and watching sports. There are many other fathers who, while far from perfect, are striving to be a true Father to their kids, teaching and training them to be the men and women they should become.

Many struggle to view God as a Father because their own experience with what a father is like has been skewed, especially if the earthly father was abusive. God declares He will be the Father to the fatherless. He will defend the widows of those whose husbands have died or abandoned them. The world may not show it, but God takes special interest in those who are without fathers. He describes true religion as taking care of widows and orphans (James 1:27) - those without fathers.

God established numerous roles of a Father, each of which He demonstrates by example. He is the head of his household, responsible for how it all turns out, for good or ill. He is responsible for providing for and protecting the family. He is responsible for the instruction of the children and preparing them for their own adult lives. He is the ultimate role model in the home as the dream of nearly every boy is to be like his daddy. The father is responsible for defending his family from people, ideas, and behaviors which are not of God. God carries out each of these and more perfectly and shows how fathers should be with their families.

Are you a father? Go to your Heavenly Father to get the help and wisdom you need to lead your family. Is your father still in your life? Honor and respect him, even if he did a poor job, because he is your father. Are there children without fathers around you? Consider becoming a father to them. We have many teachers, but few fathers. Men, be the father you are supposed to be. Women, support the father in all he needs to do. He needs you. Children, your father is trying his best. Do what you can to help him out in his job. God is the Father of all fathers and He will do His job perfectly.

Chapter 23: Forgiver

"For You, Lord, are good, and ready to forgive,
And abundant in mercy to all those who call upon You."
~Psalm 86:5

One of the powers of the President of the United States and the governor of each state is the power of pardons. A convicted criminal can appeal for a pardon, and the president or governor can grant the pardon right up to the moment when the execution is about to begin. A pardon is more than just a release from prison or the execution chamber, but a declaration of "innocent" on the charges which incarcerated that person.

This is only an incomplete picture of how God forgives our sin. Because God is a righteous and holy God, He has to completely punish sin. He cannot let a single one slide, or He would not be righteous nor just. Yet He found a way to pardon the sinner while not letting the crime go unpunished.

In the parable of the unmerciful servant in Matthew 18, the master called in a servant who had a large debt, and he simply forgave the debt. The debt did not go away. The master chose to cover it himself. He took the loss. The servant could not repay it and never would be able to. Yet the master could pay that debt out of his own pocket.

God forgave our sin and chose to take the debt we owed Him upon Himself. Jesus took that debt and willingly bore the entire wrath of God on that cross. He never sinned nor owed any debt Himself, but He became the very essence of sin on that cross and God crushed Him under His wrath. Thus we, the sinners, are able to be pardoned and yet the debt we owed is paid off. Only Jesus could do that because everyone else owes God the same unpayable debt. One already in debt cannot pay off the debt of another because he would need to pay off his own first. Only one who had no debt could pay for someone else.

God forgave our sin and no longer holds us accountable to that sin. Jesus took care of that. But there is another part of the parable. That very same servant had another servant with a tiny debt in comparison and refused to let him pay it off, let alone forgive it. How small are the sins against us compared to our own sin against God? They are not even comparable. Yes, what the other person did was wrong, but how often do we want mercy when we do something wrong? Let us not forget that God is a just God and the avenger. He will not let the sin go unanswered for.

Forgiveness is actually part of the healing process. If we refuse to forgive, we keep opening up the wounds against us and letting the poison fester. Holding grudges and getting bitter never helps us, and if it's been held for some time, it is hard to let go, especially if the wound is deep. Forgiveness will let the wound heal. It will leave a scar, but it's better to have a scar than an open wound. Do not let those who have harmed you control you by holding a grudge against them. Forgive them and let God handle making the wrong right.

Chapter 24:
Gives Discipline, Chastises

"It is good for me that I have been afflicted,
That I may learn Your statutes."
~Psalm 119:71

In the movie *Miracle,* U. S. Hockey coach Herb Brooks watches as his team is checking out the girls in the stands rather than watching and focusing on the game currently being played. After the game, he makes the team skate back and forth across the rink to the point of complete exhaustion and to where some of them could hardly stand any further. This went on until the team captain, Mike Eruzione, recognized that he no longer played for his college team but for the United States of America. This team unified and upset the USSR, who had that same year destroyed the NHL All-Stars and this same team 10-3 a couple of weeks prior. Now, this scene is debatable as to whether it actually happened or not, but the point is that Coach Brooks had to discipline his team so they would be conditioned with the endurance and perseverance to outskate the greatest team on ice.

Discipline is given a negative connotation today because it means pain and suffering. In any sport, the athletes will spend hours upon hours practicing and straining their bodies so that on the day of the competition or the game, they are able to perform to their full extent to the very end of the event. They may hate the hours of practice. They may despise the screaming of the coaches seeking to straighten them out. But they also know the end result and that is what they strive for.

God disciplines His children because He sees a discrepancy between where each of us are now and where He wants us to be. The discipline is for the purpose of training both the body and the mind to be conformed into the image of Christ. In each and every one of us, there is foolishness which is predominately the sinful nature still kicking around. God will not simply yank it out because He'll lose a lot of good stuff with it. It's the same reason goldsmiths do not hammer away impurities in the gold ingot. They melt it and because gold is so heavy, impurities will float to the surface, and he can simply scrape them off while retaining the pure metal.

God disciplines both individuals and groups. Sometimes, in order to get the attention of the group, there is one who has to "take the hit." Teachers understand this. Sometimes they need to send a student to the office in order to retain order in the class. God did this when he struck down Uzzah for touching the Ark (2 Samuel 6) and Ananias and Sapphira for lying (Acts 5).

Do not dread God's discipline. The pain is only for a moment, but the results are always worth it. Focus on the destination, not the immediate pain. God never disciplines out of anger or wrath, but out of love and with a purpose. Trust Him to take you to that destination so when it comes time to be put on display, you can demonstrate God's glory to the whole world.

Chapter 25:
God of Hosts, Lord of Hosts

"O Lord God of hosts,
Who is mighty like You, O Lord?
Your faithfulness also surrounds You."
~Psalm 89:8

Stars are amazing things to behold. Some of them are so big they could all but swallow our whole solar system. Betelgeuse, part of the Orion Constellation, is twice as large as the earth's orbit around the sun. One of the largest stars we've found, Canis Majoris, is larger than Saturn's orbit around the Sun. These are just individual stars we've found. The galaxies are amazing sights of beauty.

The Bible often compares angels to stars. Bright, majestic, glorious, and they dwarf us in both size and power. Yet, the God of the Bible is the God of Hosts, the Lord of Hosts. He made the stars as a mere afterthought on Day 4 of Creation. The angels who have such great power they could rule the whole world without much effort submit to doing only God's will. Twice in Revelation, John fell before the angel showing him the visions of the end times, and both times the angel refused worship.

Lucifer was perhaps the greatest of all the angels God created. He sought to get praise and worship for who he was and then led a rebellion, drawing 1/3 of the angel hosts with him and against God. His coup failed and he has been hell-bent on getting revenge by going after God's most-prized creation: mankind. Yet in all his rebellious efforts, even he is forced into submission to God's authority. God did not let

Lucifer, also known as Satan or the devil, take Job's body initially, then God did not let Satan take Job's life. Satan can only act within the boundaries God lets him have.

If all the stars move and operate according to the commands God gave them, how much more so should we move and operate according to God's commands? God rules over the entire universe, and nothing moves or takes place without His knowing or His allowance. God is big; He is mighty; He is powerful; He holds the entire universe within the palm of his hand. We need to take God far more seriously than we do. He is a big, ferocious God. His power and might make these stars look like nothing. He is ruler over them all, and yet he cares for each and every one of us individually and collectively.

If God is so big and so powerful to rule over the stars and limit the demons in what they can do, why do we fear these tiny problems we face? Is God not big enough for them? Many of us treat our problems as bigger than God because we do not believe He is able to handle them. We do not believe He can handle them because we do not turn to Him to solve them. He cares for us, even in the little things. He rules the entire universe, and you are His child. As Oswald Chambers has said, "He'll tax every star and every grain of sand to assist you." Turn to him.

Chapter 26: Good

"Praise the Lord!
Oh, give thanks to the Lord, for He is good!
For His mercy endures forever."
~Psalm 106:1

Paul Washer described a time he was speaking at an event with an expected hostile audience and so he primed them with anticipation of the "most terrifying truth" in Scripture. He built it up, getting the audience on the edge of their seats and then he said this: "The most terrifying truth in Scripture is this: God is good." The audience shrank back in confusion. Washer continued, "It is terrifying because God is good and we are not." He then began to explain how a good and righteous and holy God must deal with and punish sin.

Many people do not understand what it means to be good, because they get the idea that "good" is whatever gives them happiness. There is a false teaching going on that switches "God is good" with "Good is God." God is not defined by what we think is good. Good is defined by who God is and what He does. This means His love is good, His wrath is good, His justice is good, and His holiness is good. A good judge will see that crimes are punished appropriately according to the law. A corrupt judge will let the criminal off the hook. God is a good God, which means He will make sure all that is wrong is made right. The problem for us is that we have all committed treachery against the Lord of Glory. That is what sin is: treachery. As a good God, He cannot let that slide.

In His goodness and His mercy, He provided an escape route through Jesus Christ and the cross. Jesus took the punishment for sin upon Himself so that we might be reconciled to God. God was able to justify the sinner and still be righteous and punish sin. It is known as the scandal of grace. He is a good God.

But if God is so good, why do bad things happen? God gave us the freedom to choose to obey Him or not. The problem does not lie on God for bad things happening; it lies on us. The real question we have to ask is: If God is truly so good and righteous, why has He not wiped us all out by now?

God is a good God, and we can always count on Him being good. That means if He has to discipline us, it is for good. If He blesses us, it is for good. He may have to take us through a storm, but He has good reasons behind it. He let Joseph get kidnapped by his brothers, sold into slavery, falsely imprisoned, and then forgotten in prison, for the good of raising him to be the second in command in Egypt and thus saving his family from a deadly famine. Joseph saw the whole picture, which is why he was able to forgive his brothers for what they did to him.

We can celebrate the goodness of God in knowing that the wicked will be brought to justice one day. Let us not blame God for what seems to go wrong in our lives, and instead seek Him to find out how He may use that wrong for good. It does not make the wrong good, but the wrong can be used for good. God is a good God.

Chapter 27: Grace, Blessings

"But You, O Lord, are a God full of compassion, and gracious, Longsuffering and abundant in mercy and truth."
~Psalm 86:15

One of the most frustrating things for any employee of a company is to be assigned a task and not given the resources nor authority nor time to get the job done. Sometimes, what is given is the bare minimum if corners are cut and if there are no errors. Employees who are given this treatment often get the sense that their boss expects them to fail and perhaps is looking for a reason to fire them. The good bosses, however, will treat their employees well. When they assign a task, they will give that employee everything that is needed to complete the task including funds, possibly a promotion, assistance, time, and often will provide more than what is necessary for the job. Many people do not think of it this way, but this is actually what grace is.

Grace is often defined as "getting what we do not deserve" or "unmerited favor" and almost always in a good context. It is the favor of one toward another, offered at the will of the giver. It is the parent or grandparent doting on their children or grandchildren. But grace extends to a deeper meaning than this. It is empowerment. Grace gives someone the power, the authority, and the equipment to accomplish what is desired.

God is the same way in carrying it out, but He does so perfectly. He knows each of our needs (different than our wants), and He will provide for them. It may not come in the form we'd prefer. God gave Israel manna for 40 years. He used ravens to feed Elijah. John the Baptist lived on wild honey and locusts. He owns the cattle on a thousand hills. He will provide, and it is by grace that He will do so.

He has also given us a job to do to go out and make disciples of all nations. He has provided everything we need for the task. He provides for the necessary education, which comes in forms beyond the institution. He provides the finances as needed, sometimes literally at the last second. He provides manpower and organizational backing. Sometimes, He sends without such backing promising to back up the missionary Himself. He even provides difficult life experiences to prepare us for the tasks ahead. He knows exactly what is needed and never leaves anyone short.

God is a gracious God. All we need to do is ask in faith for what we need for the job at hand. We are not to ask greedily, but often we have not because we ask not. God gives us impossible tasks, and He wants us to see that they are impossible without His power and His resources. He is gracious to give us more than we would need. George Mueller lived without asking a single person other than God about his needs, and yet God provided so much he raised 1000 orphans and sponsored numerous missionaries. It is all the grace of God. Ask for it; He will give it.

Chapter 28: Great

"Great is the Lord, and greatly to be praised;
And His greatness is unsearchable."
~Psalm 145:3

Who is the greatest baseball player? Many would suggest Babe Ruth. Who is the greatest basketball player? Many people debate between Michael Jordan and Lebron James. Greatest sports team overall? Yankees, Cowboys, Steelers. Best movie of all time? Best President? Best song? Best band? Best video game? These debates are all over the place. Some find them fun; some find them boring. Even Jesus' disciples had this debate about which of them was the best and the greatest. Jesus just laughed at them.

We love celebrity status, but there is only one who truly deserves a celebrity status: God Himself. God is a great God. He is the greatest. He is not an average God nor a poor God. He is not even just a "good" God. He is a great God. He is the superlative of every term used to describe Him. He never has an "off" day. When the best pitcher in the league gives up four homeruns when he typically barely allows a single run against him, the media says, "He's only human." God never has a dud performance. He does everything perfectly.

God's knowledge is the greatest. His power is the greatest. He has the most commanding presence. His love is the greatest. His hatred is also the greatest. His righteousness is the greatest. His wisdom and teaching are the best. Nothing remotely comes close to Him. None can compare to the greatness of our God. Name anything that man can do, and God will top it. The only thing God cannot do is violate His character. He never lies, never deceives, cannot be bribed nor corrupted, and His reign will never end.

Whenever Paul tried to describe God in his letters, he always seemed to ramble on because he simply could not find sufficient words to describe how great God is. God's own name was considered so holy and so above and beyond man's comprehension that after Moses gave His name as "I AM THAT I AM," the Israelites would not even say His name lest they offend it. Whenever they made a copy of Scripture, they would purify themselves right before writing His name. If a single mistake was made, that whole page had to be burned.

God is hardly ever the greatest thing on our minds. Why do we so often treat God with such a ho-hum, nonchalant mindset? It is because in our finite, let alone sinful, nature, we simply cannot comprehend what God is truly like. We like to sing about the greatness of our God, but we really don't understand what that means. He should be the first thing on our minds, the very thing that consumes our every thought and every moment. There should be nothing that excites us more or drives our motivations and discussions more than Him. He is the greatest of all things, the name above all names. He will not play second fiddle. So let us give Him the place He deserves in our hearts: the #1 place. Everything else will fall into place the moment we do that.

Chapter 29:
Hatred of Evil

"For You are not a God who takes pleasure in wickedness,
Nor shall evil dwell with You.
The boastful shall not stand in Your sight;
You hate all workers of iniquity."
~Psalm 5:4-5

One pastor shared a story about an encounter with snakes. He *hates* snakes. When he found the snake, he did not speak gently to it and kindly ask it to go away. He did not put it in a snake cage to keep under his control. Instead, he pinned the head down, took a hoe, and cut its head off, enjoying every second of watching it die. Many people have the same reaction to spiders or that lone mosquito. There is a hunt for it, and that critter is going to die no matter what it takes.

God is a God who hates evil. He hates all sin and every form it comes in. That should frighten us, because each of us has sinned and many of us still do it because we like it. God does not tolerate sin nor turn a blind eye to it. He is ever moving and constantly working on driving sin out of us. He will take His time because He does not want to lose the good stuff he would if He rushed the job. But take note. The life of a Christian on this earth is not about getting out of hell and into heaven. It is about saving as many as possible from the wrath of God to come and to work out that salvation in fear and trembling. Paul Washer puts it this way: "If you claim to have a new relationship with God, do you have a new relationship with sin?" He is asking, if you think you are getting closer to God, does your hate and disdain for sin increase with it? It is impossible to love God and not love what he loves nor hate what he hates.

God is going to pour out His wrath upon the wicked, and He is holding back that wrath as long as He can, ever calling us to repentance. The window for repentance is waning more and more. Because He is a just God, His patience has a limit before He must execute judgment. He cannot let a single person into His presence as long as there is sin involved. His holiness and His purity are so great that combined with His hatred for sin, His mere presence would destroy that sin and all associated with it. Jesus bore the full wrath of God and became sin on that cross. At that moment, God hated Jesus with all He was and crushed Him, because He had become sin itself. It pleased the Father to crush Jesus on that cross. But it did not end there as Jesus' resurrection followed three days later.

Do we hate sin? Many of us do, except we hate it in others, and not so much in ourselves. We still must call sin out for being sin, but why are we doing so? Just to be judgmental and put someone below us, or because we genuinely care for that person, knowing that sin is going to destroy them? It helps if we looked at our own sin the same way. Do we hate our own sin as God hates it? Proverbs 8:13 declares that the fear of the Lord is the hatred of evil. Do we honor and respect God enough to hate evil? If we do not hate sin, we do not fear God, nor do we honor nor worship Him. Let us return to God. The first thing we must do is to hate the evil that pulled us away from Him to begin with. Let us hate sin as God does.

Chapter 30: Healer

"O Lord my God, I cried out to You,
And You healed me."
~Psalm 30:2

Two parents grieved at the doctor's report. Their son, only four months old, got suddenly sick. The doctors had no explanation and they said to pray. The parents prayed and their church prayed. The child made a dramatic recovery, and to this day the doctors cannot explain what happened. That child grew up to write this book.

God is the healer, the master physician. He created each and every one of us and know the number of hairs on our head. He also knows every cell, every DNA strand, and every disease which has come across mankind. God will heal some and then He won't heal others. Jesus had days where He healed the whole crowd, and other days, He only healed one person. In a couple of cases, Jesus healed a person for the purpose of proving a point to skeptics. How or why God heals some and not others is not for us to know.

Our physical bodies are temporary and will perish at some point anyway. So, whether we died today, tomorrow, or 80 years from now, it is nearly irrelevant compared to eternity and the uncorrupted, resurrected bodies we will have then. God heals for a purpose, and it can be because He is not done with that person, or because people around that person need to see Him in action. Sometimes God lets people get sick for the purpose of using that sickness as a witnessing tool of His faithfulness. But sometimes, He lets people get sick because it is a consequence of bad choices. It is not formulaic but only in accordance with God's master plan.

God never promised physical healing to everyone, but as the master physician, He asks us to seek Him when we get sick. Asa got a foot disease and instead of turning to God, he turned to the physicians and he died from it as a result. Hezekiah got a fatal disease too, and he immediately turned to the Lord for an answer. God added fifteen years to his life.

Some of the greatest disappointments take place when someone presumes God is going to heal by asking Him and He does not heal. Unless God specifically revealed He would heal in this situation, He is under no obligation to heal. David prayed for his sick child for a week before the child died, and his prayer was not answered (2 Samuel 12). But David was not presumptuous about God's healing.

God is the healer. If you get sick, go to Him first and get the statement from Him about what to do about it. God is not against going to doctors, but He is against going to them first instead of Him. If God says, "You will make it," you can walk into that doctor's office with full confidence of being healed either supernaturally or through natural means and be a blessing to those around you. If God says, "You won't make it out of this one," then you can still walk in with full confidence that God has control over the situation and still be a witness. Even if God does not heal, trust Him anyway.

Chapter 31: Hears and Answers Prayer

"I love the Lord, because He has heard
My voice and my supplications."
~Psalm 116:1

God is a God who hears and answers prayers. He is not a distant God who cannot hear nor will not hear. In 1 Kings 18, Elijah challenged the prophets of Baal to a duel where each would call to their respective god and the one who answers by fire is the real God. The prophets of Baal tried all day long in all their rituals, crying louder and cutting themselves, and nothing happened. Elijah knew what was going on, so he mocked them. He suggested Baal was sleeping or away on a trip or even using the bathroom. Nothing happened. Yet when Elijah called upon his God, fire immediately came down. God answered Elijah's prayer.

But Elijah was not a special man with special powers. He was just a man just like any other person. James 5:15-18 makes this clear. Fervent prayers of a righteous man are what get answered. Many people have this idea that prayer is just a plea for help in times of trouble. While prayer certainly can take this form, this is not all prayer is. Prayer is communication with God, pleading with Him to accomplish what He desires.

God loves fervent prayers, prayers of desperation and energy. David Brainerd is reported to have spent one day in prayer in more than waist-high snow and by the time he was done, he had melted all the snow around him from the heat of his prayers. John "Praying Hyde" Hyde prayed with such fervency that his heart literally shifted from one side of his chest to another. This man had the audacity to ask for one soul a day during one year of revival in India, then two a day, then four a day. Rees Howells was in Africa during a plague and was encouraged by God to ask that not one person would die on his property, and no one did. His prayers later were among many which were influential in turning the tides of the battles of World War II. George Mueller set out prove that one could run a ministry using absolutely nothing to support it financially than prayer. He raised over 1000 orphans without ever telling any person other than his immediate staff the financial needs, because God answered his prayers. He was also a significant financier of Hudson Taylor in China.

God loves persistent prayers, the kind where people will not quit nor let go until it is answered. Jacob illustrated this by wrestling with God all night (Genesis 32) and refused to let go even when asked until he got what he was after. Elijah knew God was going to send rain, so he prayed seven times until the answer came (1 Kings 18). Rain did not come after 1, 2, 5, or 6 times but after seven.

God answers the prayers of His saints, but He asks that we pray His way. If we would pray according to God's will, to seek God's kingdom not our own, with fervency, and not stop praying until it is done, then we would see our prayers answered.

Chapter 32: Helper

"I will lift up my eyes to the hills –
From whence comes my help?
My help comes from the Lord,
Who made heaven and earth."
~Psalm 121:1-2

Help comes from God. David needed help. He was pursued by numerous enemies. He was an outlaw in the kingdom despite doing nothing to warrant King Saul's wrath. Yet God preserved him through 21 recorded assassination attempts. God was his help and his hope.

Many people accuse Christians of using God as a crutch. They mock Christians of being too weak that they need God and cannot make it on their own. The Christian, however, knows he is too weak to make it in this world. The skeptic is too proud to admit it. If a Christian were truly honest and actually living as a Christian should live, God is not a crutch as much as He is life support. True Christianity as demonstrated by Jesus Christ is 100% God-dependent for every aspect of life. Jesus did nothing unless He saw His Father doing it, and He did not say anything unless He heard His Father saying it.

During the Last Supper, Jesus told his disciples that He would have to leave them, but He would not leave them alone (John 14). He would send a helper, the Holy Spirit. The Holy Spirit is who enabled Jesus to do what He did, and He is what makes the Christian what he is supposed to be. Christianity is not a mere religion of intellectual doctrines and feel-good statements. It is a real identity and comes with actual power.

Man is not meant to try to function without God in him. Everything man tries to do in his own strength is going to fail sooner or later. Everything man does with God leading, directing, and empowering will be successful and do its job. God is the fuel that makes the man work properly as oil and gas are to engines. But God is more than just the fuel; He is also the driver. He knows how much to hit the gas, how much to brake, where to turn, and how to make that engine run with perfect efficiency. When God runs "the man," the man functions and operates to its true intended purpose.

God is more than a helper. He does not get second bidding. He gets the headlines. He is our help and our enabler, but He is also the leading actor. He is the hero of the story. Man is the "damsel in distress." God does more than be the one who comes to man's aid and watches him go on. He goes with him. Man is sent to do impossible tasks, and God wants to go with him. The shepherd is the helper, the manager, the protector, and the provider of the sheep. Likewise, God is the helper, the manager, the protector, and the provider of the Christian. In the end, it is God who gets the praise and the attention.

Chapter 33:
Holy

"But You are holy,
Enthroned in the praises of Israel."
~Psalm 22:3

God is holy, but not just holy; He is holy, holy, holy. He is unique, separated from all the other gods. The gods of all the cultures around Israel were similar to each other. They had images of physical bodies, had physical needs to be met, had limited rule over certain domains, and ultimately had wills easily "manipulated" by the priests. The God of the Bible is not like them. He is holy. He gave the wicked king Ahab two victories against Syria (1 Kings 20) simply because they boasted that God was god of the hills but not god of the valleys. Instead, God showed He was God over both the hills and the valleys, as well as all of the creation.

God pulled Abraham out of his home where he grew up in Ur and from where his father settled in Haran alone to begin a people to himself. This nation would live by different principles, with a different sort of government, and with a unique moral code, all of which would not only separate them from the other cultures but also be a picture and a foreshadow of the Messiah.

God is not of this world. His kingdom is not a political nor social kingdom but a spiritual kingdom. God purposes to do things opposite of how man would normally do things simply to prove how unique and holy He is. He uses the weak to shame the strong, the uneducated to shame the wise, the poor to show the weaknesses of wealth, sheep to overcome wolf packs, and so on.

That which the world calls weak, God uses to make strong so that His name would be glorified and so no man can boast in his own abilities. He is holy and unique. His Holy Scriptures are unique in many ways from how they were constructed, preserved, distributed, and even in how they are attacked. The Bible is unique in its fulfillment of prophecy and its honesty. No other book of antiquity, religious thought, or any other document can remotely compare to the Bible. It is holy. It is unique and stands out from every other book.

Christianity itself is holy. It is the only religion in which man's redemption is by grace through faith, not by works. It is the only religion where God comes to man to meet man's needs rather than making man come to God by his own abilities. It is the only religion that advances with a peaceful demonstration of power, rather than by force of the sword or the gun. It is the only religion that grows and strengthens when persecution attempts to stomp it out. It is the only religion where God came to reveal Himself instead of making man search for Him.

God is a holy God, a unique and God with no comparison. All the terms and words man can use to describe Him fall painfully short of giving Him his due justice. Even the seraphim worship him nonstop saying, "Holy, holy, holy." He is holy.

Chapter 34: Honor, Honorable

*"Honor and majesty are before Him;
Strength and beauty are in His sanctuary."
~Psalm 96:6*

God is the only being worthy of all honor and praise. The Apostle John witnessed a scene in Revelation 5 of many who attempted to break the seal of a scroll and all failed. None proved worthy. Yet a small lamb, a lamb that had been slain, approached and broke the seal because He and only He was worthy. That lamb was Jesus Christ. He is the only one worthy of all honor and glory.

God spent Job 38-41 demonstrating His own power while showing Job he really had no business trying to dictate to God how to run things. He is not a small nor wimpy God. He is a great God worthy of all honor. He is the only one who could create this universe. He is the only one who can save it from the mess man has made of it.

Man in his sinful-cursed body is not capable of honoring God as He ought to be honored. The finite cannot comprehend the infinite except in how the infinite reveals itself. Man has only received snapshots of who God is in how He has performed, which is why He has so many names, descriptions, and attributes. God knows we cannot honor Him as He ought to be honored, however, He expects us to honor Him with everything we have. What we have to offer is small and often worthless, but He will accept it. How can we honor God? With obedience. To obey God is better than sacrifice or worship (1 Samuel 15:22). The way we can honor God is simply by obeying Him.

But God is not just worthy of all honor, He is also honorable. He is a God of good, noble character. He is perfectly consistent, never once going back on His word, always trustworthy and dependable, and always working to make that which is wrong right. God does not expect us to worship and honor Him merely because He is God (though we should anyway). He expects it because what He does is deserving of worship and honor. He provides life, food, shelter, and clothing. He watches over even the little details, and He reigns and rules with wisdom, righteousness, and justice. He plans everything out to work out for the good of those who love Him and are called according to His purposes (Romans 8:28). He brings justice upon the wicked, vindicating the righteous.

God is honorable. His motives, intentions, and actions are pure. He is worthy of all honor and praise and the only one worthy to receive it. He will also see He gets it one way or another.

Chapter 35: Hope

"For You are my hope, O Lord God;
You are my trust from my youth."
~Psalm 71:5

Hope is something few people have any more. The world has been fast heading toward utter chaos and anarchy, and politicians appear to be more and more complicit in the chaos rather than actually doing something about it. Many people put their hope into politics, and when one election does not go their way, they whine and cry as though they have no hope. The Christian, however, does not have to worry about the political and social scene because they have hope beyond any political figure or celebrity championing their cause. The hope of a Christian is found in God.

Hope is the anticipation that something not seen in reality now will become reality. Hebrews 11:1 uses hope to describe faith: "the substance of things hoped for." Hope is the longing for reality to change for the better. For many, hope is blind, just wishful thinking. This is when someone would like to see something happen, but they really do not expect it to happen for them. Or they make no choices or take no action to prepare for its arrival or to see it through. It is blind when there is no basis for the hope, or the object of hope has no history of fulfilling the desire.

The Christian, however, should put his hope in Christ. He is seated at the right hand of the Father upon the throne of grace ever interceding on behalf of His people. Those whose hope is in the Lord have a hope which is not only realistic but also a continual reality. Those who have learned how to "pray through" not only know how to pray the prayers God initiates, but also to have such a hope that they pray until the answer is given. Once the answer arrives, even if they do not see the answer in reality immediately, they know they can stop praying.

Both Elijah and Jehoshaphat understood this. In 1 Kings 18, after calling fire from heaven, Elijah prayed for rain seven times. His servant saw a cloud the size of a man's fist and even though there was no rain, Elijah knew his prayer was heard. In 2 Chronicles 20, Jehoshaphat prayed for help against three armies and God sent an answer. Even though the physical enemies were still around, Jehoshaphat believed the answer given and sent his singers to lead the army where they witnessed all three enemy armies defeat themselves. They had hope, and their hope was in their God. When their prayers were answered, they did not fret, even if the answer was not reality just yet. They celebrated because they knew God had heard them and the answer was coming. They had hope.

God is the hope for all mankind. He is the only one who can offer true hope and the only one who can come through on that hope. Those who put their hope and their trust into Him have never been left wanting.

Chapter 36: Horn of Salvation

"The Lord is my rock and my fortress and my deliverer;
My God, my strength, in whom I will trust;
My shield and the horn of my salvation, my stronghold."
~Psalm 18:2

God is the horn of salvation. In the Old Testament times, when this Psalm was written, horns were extremely valuable. They were used for playing music such as old-school trumpets, they were used in war for issuing commands, they were used at the gates (public squares) to make announcements, and they were used for anointing with oil.

When Joshua marched around Jericho, the people were meant to march quietly for most of the journey, yet seven priests were to blow trumpets of ram's horns. Then on the seventh time on the seventh day, they were to make a long blast and the people were to shout. The horns were the instrument to signal the call to shout. When the people shouted, God brought the walls down and the city was taken.

When God reduced Gideon's army down to 300 soldiers, the plan was to surround the Midianite camp with little else but torches and ram's horns. What is unique about this tactic is that typically only army commanders and officers could carry the horns. Why? Because if a regular soldier were to have one, he could blow the horn and give a very different order than the commanders wanted. So here there were 300 of Gideon's men, each giving the appearance of being a much larger force. Now, God instilled fear into the hearts of the Midianites as revealed by the dream of the loaf of bread destroying the tent by a Midianite solider, however, the horn indicated a position of rank and of a leader. This is part of what led Midian into a mass panic.

The gate of a city was the public square where all the people met to hear announcements, where the city council met, where grievances were heard, and where the activity took place. A horn was often used to call for people's attention. With certain blasts, it would signal what type of attention was needed, whether to assemble for a meeting, or whether an invading army was approaching, or to make a simple announcement.

Samuel came to the house of Jesse in Bethlehem, and he carried a horn of oil with him. The oil was to anoint God's next chosen king of Israel and to establish the dynasty which would culminate with Christ. When Aaron was anointed at the first High Priest, Moses poured the oil over his head to the point of flowing down his clothes and down his beard. The horn is what was used to anoint him.

God is the horn of salvation. He is the one who proclaims salvation for men. He is the one who signals the move to advance and rout the enemy. He is the one who anoints His chosen people for His tasks. He is both the user of the horn and also the horn itself. He is the horn of salvation.

Chapter 37: Humble, Humility

"And in Your majesty ride prosperously because of truth, humility, and righteousness;
And Your right hand shall teach You awesome things."
~Psalm 45:4

God is majestic because of truth, humility, and righteousness. It is difficult to associate leadership, glory, and fame with humility. There are so few examples of such behavior today. One Biblical character and one modern character both displayed high level of leadership alongside great humility: Moses and George Washington.

Moses was considered the humblest man alive. He knew full well to lead a nation of a million or more people was impossible in his own strength. He knew going with God was the only option. George Washington had an air about him which demanded utmost respect, but he never commanded that respect. When it was unanimous who was to be the first president, Washington didn't want it. He never actually ran to get elected.

Nobody exhibited humility more than Jesus. He knew He was God and did not consider it arrogant, or robbery, to be equal with God. Instead, while being God, He humbled Himself not just to take the form of a man but subjected Himself even to a criminal's death (Philippians 2:7). He also left His perfect, sinless existence to take the form of a man and dwell in the presence of sin. Even the air He breathed reeked of the curse due to Adam's sin. He lived subjected to the cursed conditions, and then in the ultimate humiliation, He hung naked in public on the very instrument of death which the word "excruciating" comes from. Public nudity was considered the greatest humiliation to a Jew, and Jesus had to bear that while dying a criminal's death. Yet through that humiliation, Jesus was raised to the right hand of the Father and given the name above all names. He already had those titles, but His actions here on earth validated them.

God is a humble God who does not flaunt His power in an egotistic manner. His self-worth is not hurt when man does not worship Him, though His wrath will be kindled. He will stoop down to take a hit He does not deserve to pull us up out of the mire. He will get Himself dirty to save one person. In the parable of the prodigal son, the son returned to the father covered in the filth of a pigsty, which was another great humiliation of a Jew. The father did not chastise him nor scold him. He covered him with a robe, and even though the son had squandered his inheritance, the father gave him his own. The father let the filth of the son come upon him, kissing him even before he got a bath and cleaned up.

This is how God is. He gets dirty and lets the sin of man get over Him as he is cleaned up. However, in the dirtiness, God is in the process of cleaning it up. He never lets it stay. He will take man as he is, but He will never leave him as he is. He will take each dirty, sinful, black-hearted, wicked person and transform him into a startling image of Christ. That is humility. He is a humble God.

Chapter 38: Instructor for War

"Blessed be the Lord my Rock,
Who trains my hands for war,
And my fingers for battle."
~Psalm 144:1

There is a great war over the souls of men. Satan has waged war against God, and his ultimate goal is to unseat Him from His Throne. However, he lost his initial coup, so he is going after God's most precious treasure: mankind. Every person is caught up in this war, whether they realize it or not. They are manipulated into being Satan's puppets and tools, or they have been rescued to fight for God's kingdom. There is no neutral territory in this war.

Satan fights dirty and does not fight with honor. He cheats any way he can, and it is absolutely imperative for every Christian to be a student of war as to recognize the tactics of the enemy. Not even an infant is safe from target from the enemy. Just ask Moses, Joash, or Jesus. All three had a death sentence upon them in infancy for no other reason than in attempt to wipe out the Savior. So, every parent must learn to fight for their children and then teach the children, even at a young age, how to fight this battle.

God is the ultimate instructor for war, and He lays out the equipment for battle, the armory, and the tactics of the enemy so that each Christian can know how to engage in this battle and how. In Ephesians 6:10-18, Paul lists the famous Armor of God, the core equipment for every Christian. Throughout the Bible are other weapons and tools to engage in this war such as prayer, praise, thanksgiving, forgiveness, and love. Yes, even love is a weapon in this war.

These weapons are not physical weapons like swords, guns, and bombs. They are spiritual weapons, and they are mighty for pulling down enemy strongholds (2 Corinthians 10:3-5). They engage in the unseen battles which have a tremendous effect in the physical. Jehoshaphat did his fighting on his knees when three physical armies surrounded him. God fought the battle for them, causing the three armies to wipe each other out with ambushes (2 Chronicles 20). Hezekiah was besieged by Assyria with a force of 185,000 troops (2 Chronicles 32) and he took his battle to prayer as well. In one night, the Angel of the Lord wiped out every single enemy soldier.

God also exposes the tactics of the enemy and the types of enemies. Nehemiah 2, 4, and 6 cover nine different ways that Sanballat, Tobiah, and Geshem came against Nehemiah to get him to stop building the walls. But even after the walls were built, this book that shows the enemy infiltrates allied ranks. Nehemiah 13:4-5 describes how Tobiah was not just allied but married to the daughter of the high priest, Eliashib. Many other tactics are seen through Jezebel, Saul, Esau, Haman, and other villains in Scripture. But with each tactic is a Biblical answer and the means of refuting and stopping them. Jesus defeated Satan in the wilderness not with an intellectual debate but with a citation of Scripture.

God is the great instructor for war. While we can learn from many others, none are a better instructor than God. He is worth heeding.

Chapter 39: Joy

"You will show me the path of life;
In Your presence is fullness of joy;
At Your right hand are pleasures forevermore."
~Psalm 16:11

God is a joyous God, and sadly this is a commonly overlooked attribute. He delights in His children. When Stephen gave his great speech to the Sanhedrin in Acts 7, he saw Jesus standing at the right hand of the Father. Most images of Jesus at the right hand of the Father are of Him sitting. Here He was standing. He was giving Stephen a standing ovation. Yes, that speech cost Stephen his life, but Jesus was so proud of Stephen at that moment that He stood with joy. Even though Stephen was being stoned at the time, he did not have a look of hate but one of love, asking God to not count the sin of murdering him against them.

In Acts 16, Paul and Silas were flogged in Philippi for no other reason than preaching the Gospel. Yet even in the suffering, they found their joy in Christ because they knew there was something greater to look forward to. Jesus Himself endured the cross because He knew the joy that would come after His resurrection (Hebrews 12:1-3).

Many people struggle with the idea of God being a joyous God, and part of that is due to a rightful emphasis on His wrath with sin. As long as sin is in the picture, God cannot share His joy. However, if that sin is dealt with, then God will no longer need to display wrath and judgment but Fatherly joy.

God is enjoyable. The only reason people complain that God is boring is because He interferes with their desire to sin. They say He does not let them do what they want and forces them to do what they don't want to do. That is the battle of the sinful nature versus the born-again nature. Yes, the things of God are death to the sinful self. Those in their sin are naturally inclined to rebel against God and find their happiness in sin. However, that sin can only produce happiness for a season, and it must always escalate just to retain the same high. It never is enough and those trapped by it hate it but can't get out from under it.

When the source of joy is God, then true joy is acquired because God always satisfies that craving for relationship, for joy, for love, and for others. He is always enough. Unlike happiness, joy is independent of the circumstances. God offers substance that is not fleeting and does not change on a whim but what can endure through both good times and bad. God's joy surpasses trials and hardships, and when He brings all things together in the consummation, those who have been born again and made anew in Christ will be freed from even the presence of sin that blocks the joy of God from bearing its fruit. When the Holy Spirit is in a Christian, joy comes out because that is what the Holy Spirit produces.

Chapter 40: Judge, Justice, Just

"He shall judge the world in righteousness,
And He shall administer judgment for the peoples in uprightness."
~Psalm 9:8

God is the Judge of all things. Abraham called Him this when he pleaded for the sake of Sodom and Gomorrah. God had told Abraham that He would destroy the two cities because of their wickedness, and Abraham pleaded that God would not destroy the righteous with the wicked. He was thinking specifically of Lot and his family. Yet not ten righteous could be found. So instead, God pulled Lot out of the city and waited to destroy it until he got out. But even then, Lot's wife looked back at the city, grieving and longing for what she would lose, and she was turned into a pillar of salt.

God is not going to let sin go unpunished nor leave the righteous without being vindicated. He will see all that has gone wrong made right. The laws of God must be enforced because if they are not, then God is cruel, corrupt, inconsistent, a liar, and ultimately inept. He is a righteous judge who is not biased and does not show favoritism. He cannot be bribed nor persuaded with technicalities and clever arguments. He will judge according to the law which He has established fairly and consistently.

There are some who teach that out of God's love He breaks His laws to save His children, however He cannot lay aside one attribute for another. God's love does not overrule His righteous standards. It was God's love that sent Christ to the cross. The cross is considered the scandal of grace because how can God be a just God and justify the wicked? The solution is that Christ made "substitutionary atonement." He took all that sin upon Himself as though He was the only guilty one, and because He was truly innocent, God was able to pour out His wrath upon His Son instead of man and satisfy His requirements that righteousness be met.

Many people do not like the idea of God being the Judge because they are going to face Him as the Judge. Every person is going to face God on Judgment Day and give an account for what they did with their time and resources, both believer and unbeliever. No one knows exactly what it is going to look like, but Revelation 20 states that the books will be opened and among them is the Book of Life, upon which every authentic, born-again believer's name will be written. Those whose names are in this book will have a defense attorney, Jesus Christ, their advocate who will intercede on their behalf and proclaim His blood as payment for their sins. Those whose names are not found in the Book of Life will asked to give an account with their own works and they will fail to satisfy the Law.

Justice will be done. God will not carry it out in man's timing nor in the manner he wishes. If a corrupt judge allows a criminal to go free, God will still give His justice to the criminal and the judge. He will punish the wicked, and He will reward the righteous. Every person will receive their due, so man has no need to take the law into his own hands. God is the Judge, and He will do what is right.

Chapter 41: Kindness

"Let, I pray, Your merciful kindness be for my comfort,
According to Your word to Your servant."
~Psalm 119:76

Many skeptics accuse God of not being very friendly, saying, "It's no wonder you have so few friends considering how you treat the ones you have." What are they saying? They look at the hardships and persecutions Christians go through, and they see the problems of all the people in the Bible and wonder what God is doing about it. If God were a kind and good God, He would not make His people suffer, right? Jesus did not promise an easy life; however, the Bible does describe a kind God.

The Christian understands that there is a point and purpose to every hardship. He knows that God uses those hardships to shape and mold him for His purposes, but even in that process, God is still kind. God knows precisely the amount of pressure to apply on people to make them into what He desires. He never allows any temptation to be too strong to force someone to give in, and He always provides a means to escape. While He will break and shatter someone, He does so for the purpose of rebuilding them into something far better than what they were before. God is kind enough to never allow sin to dwell in his people without dealing with it.

Kindness is one of the fruit of the Spirit of Galatians 5:22-23. It is a defining attribute of God. Like with love, kindness is defined by the action and character of God. Kindness is often paired with love, with mercy, with grace, with gentleness, and/or with compassion. It is difficult to find kindness without one of these other fruits present.

God is kind in everything He does. He protects man in more ways that we could ever know, allowing only which is necessary to bring people closer to Him. He is also not an over-protective parent. Should someone decide to run wild, if he does not belong to God, he will be allowed to go free and at some point be turned over to his sinful desires in repeated rebellion. Yet, if he belongs to God, the discipline of God will keep bringing that man back. Jacob and Esau learned this. God let both run wild, but only Jacob was constantly reeled back in.

God has no obligation to be kind to anyone. It is simply an outflow of His character. He can withhold it or pour it out on whoever He desires. It is never on a whim nor arbitrary but based on His character and His will. Sometimes the blessing or the curse is given due to a person's heart attitude. Esau despised his birthright, and even though he wept with tears when he realized he would get nothing, it was only because he would get nothing, not because he was sorry for his sin. Jacob was a mess of a man and did not actually walk God's way until he wrestled with God at age 91. But he sought and drove to get what God had. David was not exactly a moral role model either; he was not a great father, he committed adultery, and he murdered to cover it up. But no one ever sought after God's heart like he did. God showed kindness to Jacob and David but did not show it to Esau. God is kind, but sin will always block it from arriving.

Chapter 42: King, Reigns, Lord

"The Lord reigns;
Let the earth rejoice;
Let the multitude of isles be glad!"
~Psalm 97:1

God is the King. He is the true ruler who governs over the affairs of man. A king is a monarch with the ultimate authority of the realm. With the signing of the Magna Carta, the king was brought under the rule of law, so the people had a means of holding a king responsible for his actions. However, there are totalitarian dictators who think they are above the law and can do whatever they want. God is a King who submits Himself to His own laws. If God were to violate His laws, He would deny himself and that is something He cannot do. Why? Because His laws are an outflow of His character.

Jesus is not King just because He said He was king. He is the rightful king. When God established David upon the throne, He promised that a son of David would always remain on the throne. Skeptics question the integrity of that claim because with the conquest of Judah at the hands of Nebuchadnezzar, the throne of Judah remained empty. However, the promise did not say the throne would be occupied the entire time. What God promised was that David's dynasty would never end. The throne would be occupied only if the line followed God's commands. It did not, with only four notable kings seeking the Lord: Asa, Jehoshaphat, Hezekiah, and Josiah. But the line was never wiped out (despite getting down to a single person with Joash and Sheltiel, son of Jehoiachin). Four hundred years later, Jesus, adopted by Joseph into the legal lineage of the kings and descended by blood via the line of Mary through David's son Nathan, entered the scene. Jesus is the rightful King of the Jews.

A king is responsible for overseeing the affairs under his authority. The U.S. has divided political authority into the three branches of legislative, executive, and judicial, but a king is responsible for all three branches at once. He is responsible for making the laws, enforcing the laws, and making judgments on how the laws are supposed to be enforced. The king is responsible for setting up his servants to operate his kingdom as he wants to rule it. He is to provide the infrastructure for the people to operate according to his principles. When the people rebel or break a law, the king is the one who must administer justice.

God is a king who carries out all the responsibilities of a king to perfection. He is a good king, a wise king, and a just king. He governs and reigns over all, and any area of life that is submissive to the reign of Christ is actually a peaceful area. Only by submission to Christ's rule can peace actually be achieved. He is the King, and He is the ruler no matter what anyone says. There will be no successful coup and no change of administration. He is the King.

Chapter 43:
Law Giver

"The law of the Lord is perfect, converting the soul;
The testimony of the Lord is sure, making wise the simple."
~Psalm 19:7

God is the law giver. Not *a* law giver; *the* law giver. God's laws are not meant to be a legalistic establishment where the purpose of the laws is to enforce and follow the rules. God's laws always have a purpose. The primary purpose of the Law is not to make a standard so hard that no one could actually fulfill it (though that is true), but to show what sin is and what it is not.

There is not a single person guilt-free of the Law except for Jesus Christ. He is the only one who never worshipped any god other than God, never bowed to an idol nor made one, He never used God's name as a curse word, nor misrepresented His name. He kept the purpose of the Sabbath, remembering God's work over the six days but not abandoning needs for the sake of the law. He honored and obeyed His earthly parents. He never committed murder nor hated anyone, wishing they were dead. He never committed adultery, nor looked at another person with sexual lust. He never stole anything, no matter how small, nor stole the glory of God by claiming to be Him. He never lied and He never coveted anything which God did not give Him.

In Romans 7, Paul describes how he would not know what sin was but for the Law telling him what the sin was. He treated it as a school master to define what is right and wrong. The Law was never meant to be kept by man, only to expose that he cannot meet God's perfect standards, requiring a

Savior. When man properly responds to the Law, he will realize how far he falls short of meeting it and it should send him with pleas of mercy before the feet of Jesus.

The Law has another function besides the conviction of sin. It makes even a simple person wise. Proverbs 1:7 states that the fear of the Lord is the beginning of wisdom. Little can instill a proper fear of a righteous and holy God than knowing His laws and knowing no one can even come close to fulfilling them. When one knows the standards of God and understands how God handles sin, it will make him wise to move towards doing things God's way versus doing things man's way.

God's laws are perfect, exhibiting God's perfect and holy character. They are not legalistic laws, nor are they laws intended for man to be able to fulfill. They are laws that show how far man in his sin has fallen and laws that Christ is able to fulfill. However, being born again does not free a person from the Law. Jesus did not come to get rid of the Law and make things a free-for-all. He came to carry out the Law in and through His children. Man cannot fulfill the Law, but Christ in and through man can. The Law is never to be despised because it reveals who God is, what He wants, and expresses how man desperately needs a Savior.

Chapter 44: Laughs at the Wicked

"He who sits in the heavens shall laugh;
The Lord shall hold them in derision."
~Psalm 2:4

The scoffer laughs at the things of God and mocks both Him and any who follow after Him. However, while the scoffer laughs now, it is God who laughs now and laughs last. The scoffer will not laugh for long. Voltaire was a famous atheist who proudly proclaimed that within 50 years of his death the Bible would be relegated to museum displays and thoroughly removed from society. God had something else to say. The Geneva Bible Society bought Voltaire's house after he died and filled the house to the roof with printed Bibles.

God protects His people and His book. When anyone lashes out at God, there are only two end results: that person is converted as was the case with Paul, or that person will see failure and ruin. In 2 Kings 2, Elisha had just returned from seeing Elijah being taken up in a whirlwind, and 42 young men came out mocking him, not just for his baldness but telling him to go follow Elijah up to heaven. They did not want anything to do with God's chosen prophet. Elisha cursed them for it, and God sent two bears to maul them to death. When David fled from Absalom, Shemei came to mock him, but David would not speak ill against him, thinking he may have been sent from God. When he returned, Shemei proclaimed his loyalty, and while David forgave him, he did not forget it. When he died, he gave Solomon orders to deal with him as he saw fit. David never sought revenge on his own, including during any of the 21 recorded assassination attempts on his life. Why? Because he knew that God was the avenger and would have the final say in all matters.

Man, nation, expert, scholar, scientist, psychologist, empire, and everything in between have thrown up their fist at God, raging at him while he sits on the throne. That is the nature of sin. The thumbing of the nose, the wrathful fist-shaking rebellion against Almighty God, which will not bend the knee to the Lordship of Jesus Christ. Man in his sinful nature is in constant rebellion against God and will do stupid things and that which they know is wrong for no other purpose other than not doing it God's way. God laughs at them. He knows full well how foolish it is to rebel against Him and how much damage it does to us.

How does God laugh at the wicked? He does so by using the complete opposite of how they would do things to accomplish His goals. God uses who the world calls weak. He uses the uneducated to shame the wise. He uses the poor to shame the rich. He uses small numbers to beat big numbers. He uses sheep to defeat wolves. In every way, how the world tries to strategize their best resources, God will take the rejects and beat the best with them. The wisdom of God is so far above and beyond what this world has to offer, and He makes sure that there is absolutely no way it gets done apart from Him. The wicked will rage and rail against the King of Kings, but He is the one laughing, because He knows how futile their efforts are.

Chapter 45:
Life, Living

"My soul thirsts for God, for the living God.
When shall I come and appear before God?"
~Psalm 42:2

God is life. He is not a dead god whose only connection is through a motionless statue. He is a living God. He is the source of all life. All the secular scientists talk about the evolution of the species and yet even if one were to give all their models the benefit of the doubt (despite having no actual facts to back them up), all they can give is the evolution of a physical body, but not life. Even if the physical body could "come together" on its own, life will not come as a result. The Law of Biogenesis is the only scientific law of biology, and it states that life can only come from other life. This means that the original living creatures on this earth still had to come from other life and that life was God, who spoke them all into being according to Genesis 1.

Christianity preaches Christ and Christ crucified, however if Jesus was still in a tomb, nothing would have been accomplished. The cross is accompanied with the resurrection, and it is the resurrection of Jesus that gives Christianity its power. In 1 Corinthians 15, Paul even goes on to say that if Christ was not risen, then the Christian is to be pitied among all men. The Christian faith is rooted in this idea of dying to sin and being risen to new life. That is baptism in a nutshell.

The wages of sin is death (Romans 6:23). God gave Adam and Eve a simple choice: life or death. The Tree of Life, or the Tree of the Knowledge of Good and Evil. They chose the latter, knowing that doing so would result in death. Joshua

24:15 gives a similar challenge: "Choose for yourselves this day whom will you serve… as for me and my house, we will serve the Lord." Joshua chose life.

Romans 5-7 is Paul's big argument about life and death in relation to sin and to Christ. Someone who is alive to sin is not alive to Christ, and being alive to Christ requires death to sin. The Bible speaks in terms of black and white. It is one way or the other; there is no middle ground. Every person is in transition from one extreme to the other, but no one will ever stay that way. Every person is transitioning either away from God and toward full sin and death, or away from sin and toward God. The life of sin may give pleasure for a season, but the end result is death. The life of God produces more life and kills that which produces death and decay.

1 Corinthians 15:26 describes how death is the last enemy to be destroyed. God is the God of life. He makes all that is near Him alive. But His holiness and His purity are so bright and so strong that sin and death will be annihilated in His presence. God must separate Himself from anything corrupted with sin because He will kill it because of His righteousness. Yet, He offers man a chance at life again through His Son Jesus Christ. It is available to all, not to take at convenience but at God's drawing and call. Man is responsible for responding to that call. Those who reject the call as Adam did will die. Those who receive the call will be saved and given new life. God is God of the living and asks each person to receive it lest the judgment come and reward the final doom upon those who have chosen death.

Chapter 46: Light, Lamp

"Your word is a lamp to my feet
And a light to my path."
~Psalm 119:105

God is light. Light reveals, exposes, is knowledge, gives heat, gives clarity, and defines the boundaries. Where light is not, there is darkness. Darkness hides and is ashamed. The sinful love the darkness because it hides their evil deeds, and they hate the light because it exposes them. Those who live in the light are not ashamed of the light. They have nothing to fear because any problems they have will already have been exposed and dealt with.

God is light. Light reveals the path, the way to go. Many people live in darkness not knowing which way to go. The lamps used in Bible times were not great producers of light; they often only revealed enough to take one step forward. Many times, God only provides enough light for each person to take the next step. He will let the person know what the main vision is for him but just enough to work his current step in the process to get there.

If God were to show any Christian every step of the journey he is to take before taking him on it, that Christian would never go on it. He would see all the hardships and challenges and deem them not worth it before going through it and seeing God working in and through them. Yet every Christian who has stayed faithful through those challenges and hardships never regrets them because they have seen God at work.

God never withholds light for the purpose of just blinding people. Those on their journey with God frequently go through times of fog and shadow, but sometimes those times are actually for protection. There is an enemy who is like a lion seeking whomever he can devour (1 Peter 5:8). But that enemy has limited vision. When someone is in a fog and cannot see, the enemy also cannot see them. One man prayed for God to turn on the lights and so God did; in the spirit, he saw a demonic creature sniffing around as he looked for prey. The man immediately asked God to turn the lights off. In other circumstances, God is maneuvering His people in the shadows to position them where the enemy cannot see what is happening. Then when the time for battle comes, God lifts the fog, and the enemy is caught unprepared.

God is light. After creating the heavens and the earth in a void, incomplete state, the first thing God created to bring order into the picture was light (Genesis 1:3). He left the creation with days and nights to be among the markers to identify time. However, in Revelation 21-22, He reveals that in the New Earth there is not going to be a sun to give light because God Himself is going to be the light. There will be no 'day' or 'night' because the light will shine without ceasing for eternity.

God is the one who sets the boundaries and the one who exposes all. Anything that man tries to hide from God will be exposed, but anything man exposes willingly to God will be covered by the blood of Christ. God is light, and He will expose all in due time. Nothing will be hidden, and all mysteries will made clear.

Chapter 47: Lord of lords, God of gods

"Oh, give thanks to the God of gods!
For His mercy endures forever.
Oh, give thanks to the Lord of lords!
For His mercy endures forever."
~Psalm 136:2-3

God is the Lord of lords, the God of gods, and the King of kings. Of all the rulers and deities in this world, the God of the Bible is ruler over them all. The lords and kings of men held dominion over their regions, however God was the one who put them in place, and He was the one who allowed them to continue their reign or not. He raised up Pharaoh to be the mightiest man on earth for the purpose of bringing him down and displaying His power over the strength of men. He raised up Nebuchadnezzar to punish all the nations of the Middle East. Nebuchadnezzar thought it was his own great strength and power, and God reminded him who really gave him his power the hard way in Daniel 4. Then in Daniel 5, God brought down Belshazzar from power when He wrote on the wall. He determines every ruler of every nation.

Sometimes God puts rulers in place because the people wanted to do things their own way. That is why God allowed Israel to have a king (1 Samuel 8). It wasn't who God wanted to rule but it was the one the people wanted. And yet despite their rejection of God as their ruler, He still maintained His sovereignty over them, no matter how many times they tried to get away from under Him.

God is the God over all other gods. No other deity can remotely compare to God. All the gods of the ancient near east did not act like deities but rather super-humans. They had physical bodies, had physical needs such as for food, traveled, slept, had limited domains, and 'ruled' no differently than a normal king. If one were to trace the history of the gods of these cultures, one would find they do not trace to man's ideas about God, but rather to the people and patriarchs of the pre-diluvian world and immediate post-diluvian world: the men and women who lived 900+ years as Genesis 5 and 11 record. These people were mythicized into deities, and that does not even get into the Nephilim and who they were. Yet God is the God over all of them.

He proved He was God over the Syrian gods by giving Ahab two victories, one in the hills and one in the valleys in 1 Kings 20. He silenced worship of Baal with Elijah's showdown on Mt. Carmel in 1 Kings 18. He used Shadrach, Meshach, and Abednego to endure the fiery furnace and Daniel through the lions' den to prove to the Babylonians and the Persians that He was the True God.

God is the Lord of all lords and the God over all the gods. No other can remotely compare with Him. He is the true master of this universe and rules over every ruler.

Chapter 48: Love, Lovingkindness

"Because Your lovingkindness is better than life,
My lips shall praise You."
~Psalm 63:3

God is love. In the same way that He is good, love is an innate attribute or characteristic of God. Unlike any other deity where they can be loving and they can be good, with God, love is part of His very essence. That means all of who God is defines what love is. Many people think "love is God," however that statement suggests that whatever they think love is, that is what God is like. Most of those people define "love" as allowing them to do whatever they want and not telling them "no." Yet, little could be further from the truth.

Love does not allow anyone to get away with anything. It is not tolerant of that which is harmful or destructive. Love will drive out sin, but it will do so the right way. While God is kind and gentle when He disciplines us, He does not let sin slide. For love to be love, there must be hate for anything or anyone that comes against that which is loved. A parent loves his or her child. If someone kidnaps or harms that child, the love for that child will be equally matched by the parent's hatred toward that kidnapper. While forgiveness and mercy can be offered, a righteous anger burns because of the love for that which was harmed.

It is impossible to love two opposites. Jesus said in Matthew 6:24 that it is impossible to serve two masters because one will end up ruling over the other in the individual. Which one will rule? The one that is loved. The only one that should have full love is God. He is the one who should always take precedence. Not money, not science, not reputation, not education, not anything this world cherishes. James 4:4 states that friendship with the world (or the worldly system) is enmity with God. Anyone who wants to be friends with this world's system and the way this world thinks is going to be enemies with God. It is impossible to love both.

There are preachers who have questioned what it means to love. Typically, the purpose for such a question is to muddy the waters so the command is not clear, so it does not have to be obeyed. That's exactly what the teacher of the law tried to give Jesus – to muddy the waters so he didn't have to love his neighbors. In response, Jesus gave him the parable of the good samaritan. Paul also gives a very clear description of what love is and how it looks in 1 Corinthians 13:1-8. Those who question what it means to love either have not read the Bible or are looking for a reason to not do it.

God is love and those who have been born again will bear it as a fruit of the spirit (Galatians 5:22-23). Love is the first one mentioned, followed by joy. Paul used to be the most hateful, religious zealot, but then he met Christ and became full of love. Yet in that love, he did not hold back when it comes to dealing with false teachings or anyone who would bring harm to the brothers and sisters that he met throughout Asia Minor. Paul's love for the churches he planted burned so brightly that all who brought in false teachings among them received the heat from him. Paul showcased God's love for the saints through all his letters. God is love.

Chapter 49:
Majesty

"Honor and majesty are before Him;
Strength and beauty are in His sanctuary."
~Psalm 96:6

God is a majestic God. He is full of grandeur. He is regal. He is bathed in glory. Revelation tells us that when God puts the New Earth into play, there will be no sun because His glory alone will be the light. There will not be any night. Isaiah saw the Lord in His glory in Isaiah 6, and he fell to his face saying, "Woe is me! A man of unclean lips." Daniel had a vision of a Man and was so awestruck it terrified him to almost the point of death (Daniel 10). He prayed for an answer to the vision, and it took three weeks for the angel to get through to deliver it. John saw Jesus in His glorified form and fell onto his face as though dead (Revelation 1).

In Exodus 33, Moses asked to see God's glory. He wanted to see God's majesty. God told him it was impossible because His glory would kill him, however He would allow Moses to see His backside, a shadow of His glory. He hid Moses in a rock cleft and passed by so Moses could not see Him coming but he could look after He began passing. Later in Exodus 35, Moses' face shined so brightly he had to cover it with a veil because he had been in the presence of the majestic God.

Sin has a terrible effect upon man because it prevents him from being able to see God face-to-face. The face displays the real nature of a person, particularly the eyes. The eyes of a person reveal their current mood, spirit, intent, and often what they are thinking. The eyes reveal the status of the soul. Because of sin, man's eyes reveal wickedness. Because God is so pure, holy, and majestic, if one were to look into His eyes in his sinful state, they would kill said person on the spot. Every person who witnessed the Father or the Son in Their glorified forms and lived to tell the tale are exceptions, and they knew they should be dead. Even then, none of them looked into the Father's eyes directly.

Only two people have ever seen the Father face to face: Adam and Jesus. Adam lost that privilege the moment he ate from the Tree of the Knowledge of Good and Evil. Jesus, the Last Adam, did what Adam could not, completely and fully fulfill the Law. Because Jesus did what He did on the cross, we get to receive the benefits.

One day, every Christian will get to see the Father face-to-face. That day is going to come when He brings the consummation of all things, and everyone receives their resurrected and glorified bodies. On that day, we will see the Father in all His glory and will get to spend eternity in that eternal majesty and glory. God is clothed in majesty, and when we see Him on that day, the Bride of Christ will have all eternity to not only glory in His majesty, but we'll also get the privilege of finally worshipping Him as he deserves to be worshipped. It will be a majestic and glorious day.

Chapter 50: Merciful

"Have mercy upon me, O God,
According to Your lovingkindness;
According to the multitude of Your tender mercies,
Blot out my transgressions."
~Psalm 51:1

King David had just committed the biggest atrocity of his life. He failed to go to war when he was supposed to, saw a naked woman, had sex with her, and then murdered her husband to cover it up when the husband refused to let up on his duty. Uriah was one of David's Mighty Men, one of his closest friends, one of 37 who accomplished great feats in battle. David lusted after Uriah's wife, stole her, and murdered him to cover it up. Then after the baby from that pregnancy was born, God sent Nathan the prophet to address him, giving him the famous parable of the rich man who stole a poor man's single lamb to feed a guest, and declaring, "You are the man!" (2 Samuel 11-12). Psalm 51 is David's song of repentance.

David knew who his God was and constantly called upon His attribute of mercy. David had received all the blessings of God, who took a poor shepherd boy, the youngest of a lowly family, to raise him to slay a giant and establish him as the greatest king of Israel's history. This was the blemish on David's record, and yet God granted him mercy. According to Israel's law, David should have been executed and stoned along with Bathsheba. God still gave him mercy, but not without consequences. His son, Absalom, would see to it that David's house remained full of violence and then would publicly violate David's harem. But David learned his lesson. When he was dying and his advisors gave him a young virgin to sleep with him to keep him warm, he would not do so.

God's mercy is exceedingly above and beyond what can be imagined. While He does discipline His children, even that is an act of mercy because without the discipline, each person would go further and further into sin and darkness and eventually death. In every case, when God prepared to bring judgment, there was mercy involved or available. He would have spared Sodom and Gomorrah if just ten righteous people could be found. He did not tell Jonah to tell Nineveh to repent, yet they did, and God spared them. He gave Noah instructions to build an Ark to save mankind and animals from the Flood, but the ark was big enough to support far more than eight people.

Yet, some of the mercies God offers required one "sacrificial lamb" per say. Nadab and Abihu were struck down for offering profane fire before the Lord (Leviticus 10). Uzzah was killed for touching the Ark of the Covenant because David was not having it transported correctly (2 Samuel 6). Ananias and Sapphira were struck dead for lying to the Holy Spirit (Acts 5). These were all gifts of mercy because they caused the priests, David, and the early church to repent immediately and take God much more seriously. God only had to strike one or two down instead of multitudes.

God is a merciful God, and His mercy is not to be taken for granted.

Chapter 51:
Mighty One

"The Mighty One, God the Lord,
Has spoken and called the earth
From the rising of the sun to its going down."
~Psalm 50:1

God is mighty. He is not a weak and puny God; He is a mighty God. He is great and powerful. He can do all things. He can overcome any challenge thrown at Him. He loves to do the impossible for us, and He has the might and the strength to do it.

There is nothing too hard for God. The skeptic will ask "Can God create a rock so big He cannot lift it?" Such a question is foolishness. This assumes God is limited by the forces of gravity, and in order for a rock to be too big to lift, there must be a source of gravity for that rock, which would naturally be bigger than that rock. An infinite loop then ensues as each source of gravity gets bigger and bigger and never ends. In reality, the question is flawed for two reasons. It tries to describe an infinite being by finite definitions and measurements, and it assumes God is submitted to the very laws of nature which He created.

While God is omnipotent, one thing He cannot do is violate Himself. That also means he cannot perform any logically invalid task. He cannot make a square circle, for example. But He can do many things we would determine to be impossible by natural means. He is a miracle worker.

The enemy will flaunt his power and his might advancing with great numbers and great noise. God chooses the weak things through which He displays His might. Three armies charged Jehoshaphat and when he came to face them, God sent all three into confusion and they all wiped each other out (2 Chronicles 20). Assyria sent a massive army against Hezekiah, and the Angel of the Lord wiped out 185,000 soldiers in a single night (2 Chronicles 32). God gave Gideon victory over large army of Midianites with just 300 men (Judges 7). God overthrew the most powerful nation in the world at the time when He sent the ten plagues and buried Egypt's army in the Red Sea (Exodus 7-14).

God is not just mighty enough to overcome individual situations; He is the Mighty One who overcame both sin and death. In order for Jesus to rise from the dead, He had to die. Because He conquered death, every Christian will also conquer death if and only if they are attached intimately with Christ. Each person in Christ will die as He died but also rise as He was raised (1 Corinthians 15). The same power that created the universe out of nothing but the spoken voice of God is the same power that can take a sinful wretch and transform him into a holy, pure, spotless Bride for Christ.

God is mighty, and His strength and power are unmatched. He is powerful enough to save, and He is powerful enough to enforce His law and judgment on the wicked. He will get what He wants done, and His might is so great that He can take a sinful, messed up human and still use him despite his flaws to carry out His plans. He is a mighty God.

Chapter 52: Miracle Worker

"Many, O Lord my God, are Your wonderful works
Which You have done;
And Your thoughts toward us
Cannot be recounted to You in order;
If I would declare and speak of them,
They are more than can be numbered."
~Psalm 40:5

God is a miracle worker. He loves to do the impossible to showcase His power. When Israel escaped from Egypt, God actually led them backwards to camp against the Red Sea when Pharaoh's army advanced upon them. The people thought they would die there, but God showcased His might by not only holding Egypt back with a pillar of fire but then splitting the Red Sea so Israel could cross on dry land. Then when Egypt took chase, God buried them in the sea. God is a miracle worker.

Countless miracles are recorded in the Bible. He made an old man and old woman (Abraham and Sarah) have a child. He provided water and manna for Israel for 40 years while making their clothes never wear out. He split the Jordan River while in flood stage. He brought down the walls of Jericho. He made oil and flour multiply for a widow housing Elijah. He brought down fire from heaven three times: once at Mount Carmel in 1 Kings 18 and twice when the king of Israel tried to bring in Elijah in 2 Kings 1. He made an ax head float in 2 Kings 6. He delivered Shadrach, Meshach, and Abednego from the fiery furnace.

Jesus performed even more miracles. He turned water into wine, calmed the storm, healed paralytics, cast out demons, multiplied food, walked on water, cured leprosy, healed from a distance, and raised the dead. That's not even the complete list. The Apostles performed miracles too. Peter walked on water and healed a cripple. Ananias enabled Paul to see after he had been blinded on the road to Damascus, and then Paul cast out demons. The Apostles knew their limitations and understood it was God's power and God alone who performs the miracles. While the time of a "miracle worker" has ceased, as these miracles were to demonstrate the authority these people had to speak for God, God has by no means ceased doing the miraculous.

Those who have been involved in ministry have reported instant healings, food multiplication, language translation (two men speaking completely different languages, not knowing a word of the other and getting along just fine, as happened at Pentecost), the perfect timing of events, and supernatural financial provision. The biographies of George Mueller, Rees Howells, Hudson Taylor, C. T. Studd, Amy Carmichael, and those of smaller ministries have reported such miracles. Those who seek after the Lord and believe in faith that He will deliver on what He promised will discover that He will do so. He is the God of the impossible. He is the great Miracle Worker.

Chapter 53:
Most High

"That they may know that You, whose name alone is the Lord,
Are the Most High over all the earth."
~Psalm 83:18

God is the Most High God. He has the name above all other names. He is the ultimate source of authority. There are none above Him, nor equal, nor even close to Him. Skeptics complain about the use of the Bible and its author as an ultimate authority because to do so, one must use the Bible to establish the authority of the Bible. They say that is "circular reasoning" Here is the difference between the Bible and the secular authorities when it comes to circular reasoning.

The secular authorities appeal to arbitrary authorities, using one to define and establish another, which then defines and establishes another, and it circles around. Christians reference one authority which appeals to itself. For an ultimate authority to be correct, it must be internally consistent. It also cannot appeal to any other authority, or it would not be an ultimate authority. Despite all the claims of the Bible having contradictions, it does not take very long of a deeper study to find out none actually exist and any such contradictory claims actually have nothing to do with the actual content. The Bible has passed and endured every attempt to scrutinize it and the reason why it has and always will is because it is the Word of God, the Most High Authority on all matters.

In many circles, the inerrancy of the Bible is rarely brought into question, however where one truly stands is revealed by how they answer the question of the sufficiency of Scripture and its author. If God is the Most High and His Word, the written, tangible, full expression of who He is, has highest authority, then He must also be sufficient. That means any other authority must be either discarded or be submitted to the Bible and its author. If the Bible is sufficient, that means it has the answers for every situation we face. While time, culture, and technology change, the types of events encountered never change. There is nothing new under the sun according to Ecclesiastes, which means every scenario is just a different packaging of what has already taken place or a greater/lesser form of what has already happened. The Bible has the answers to every type of situation independent of time, culture, or language.

All authorities and rulers must bow before the King of Kings. All the sciences, psychologists, political leaders, experts, philosophers, businesses, crime syndicates, etc. are under the authority of God. He is the Most High God. No Christian has to fear man because what can man do to him? Each Christian should fear God because He can do far more. Man can kill the body, but God can preserve the body until the time has come. God can take life at any moment, and He can kill the soul. What He says goes. He is the Most High God, the ultimate authority, and sufficient for all truth, knowledge, and life.

Chapter 54:
No Turning, Consistent, Constant

"The Lord has sworn in truth to David;
He will not turn from it:..."
~Psalm 132:11

There is no shadow of turning in God. He is consistent and constant. His character never changes. His standards never alter. He is not fickle. He does not claim to be our friend at one moment then abandon us at the moment of our desperation. He does not make rash vows, nor does He fail to deliver on what He promises. His ways are trustworthy, and they are trustworthy because they do not change.

God made a covenant with David that because of his loyalty and his pursuance of God's heart, God would ensure that a son of David would always remain on the throne. On David's end, his sons would need to stay loyal to God Himself to sustain it. Of all the kings who would follow, only four could be described as 'good': Asa, Jehoshaphat, Hezekiah, and Josiah. All the other kings were either totally wicked, failed to stay loyal, or failed to stop idolatry within their realms. But with each wicked king, God remembered His promise to David and retained the line of kings.

The kings of Israel went through numerous dynasties where only Jehu's line lasted up to four generations. All the others were ended through execution, assassination, suicide, or other causes. With Judah, however, while there were assassinations and a near annihilation of the royal family by Athaliah, there was always someone in the line of David.

David's dynasty did not stay on the throne, however. Manasseh was such a wicked king that God said it was enough. Josiah's repentance and revival brought a lot of people back to the faith, but he could only delay the judgment. Then Josiah's grandson Jehoiachin was cursed to have no one in his bloodline on the throne. The throne was then abolished with the Babylonian conquest; however, the dynasty did not end. The line continued, and Matthew records this line, including the legal transfer of the royal line to Shealtiel and Zerubbabel, all the way down to Joseph and his formal legal adoption of Jesus. Had the throne still been occupied, Jesus would have been raised by a political king, not a carpenter.

God kept His promise to David for the 1000 years between David and Jesus. He had every legal right to turn His back on the royal family because of their repeated returns toward sin. It was no different than in the times of the Judges. God made His promises and the people kept trying His patience. Numerous times He moved to wipe out the entire people and start over with someone else, but the intercessions of people like Moses and Josiah deterred God's wrath. God remembered His promises and did not turn from them.

God is constant. There is no shadow of turning in Him, not hint of hypocrisy or double-mindedness. He says what He means and means what He says and makes it clear so no one can be justified in twisting it. God never goes back on what He says.

Chapter 55: Oath and Covenant Keeper

"He remembers His covenant forever,
The word which He commanded, for a thousand generations."
~Psalm 105:8

God is an oath-keeping and covenant-keeping God. He fulfills His promises and never breaks them. God never makes any rash vow that He will regret later down the road. When He makes a promise, He fully intends to carry it out, and in no promise has He failed to produce. The first covenant God made was with Adam and Eve regarding how to manage the garden and to not eat from the Tree of the Knowledge of Good and Evil. But when they sinned, God told the Serpent of the One who was to crush his head (Genesis 3:15) and another covenant was established.

God made a covenant with Noah after the Flood that never again would there be a massive worldwide catastrophe as what just happened, and He gave us the rainbow to constantly remind us of that. He then set up the seasons which would never cease to cycle (Genesis 8:22). Next up was the Abrahamic Covenant and the establishment of the Jewish people. Through Abraham would not only come many nations but the Savior. David's covenant established the royal line and would eventually give Jesus the rightful throne of Israel.

The ultimate covenant God established is the New Covenant found in Christ Jesus. Adam and Eve gave man the Law of Sin and Death, legally passed on from generation to generation. The only way to avoid the penalty of death is perfect fulfillment of the Law, which is based on God's perfect standards - impossible for man to fulfill on his own. Christ came not to abolish the Law but to make it possible for man to die to that Law and be resurrected to a new law, the law of grace (Romans 7). The cross is what made that transition possible. Covenants cannot be broken by will or decree. Most often, they can only be broken by the death of one of the members. Only man can die; God cannot die and remain dead.

God keeps His covenants and holds each person to the covenants they make. This is why He warns against making rash vows and being careful about who to keep company with. He views integrity as a critical thing to maintain. He is a God of integrity, and anything He says He will do will be done.

Chapter 56: Overseer of Creation

"The waters saw You, O God;
The waters saw You, they were afraid;
The depths also trembled."
~Psalm 77:16

God is the overseer of Creation. The creation itself submits to the word and the command of God. Genesis 1 is the account of Creation. Over six days, "God said…" and it was. There was nothing except God prior to that. No matter, no energy, no heat, no light, nothing physical, nothing except God in the spiritual realm. Then everything we see today came into being in six days, then on the seventh day God rested.

All the laws of science discovered today were created by God, are upheld by God, and can be manipulated or suspended by God. Apart from Him, they do not work nor exist. He is the one who set the planets and the stars into motion. He is the one who placed the earth where it needs to be in the universe so we can use the planets and stars for both time keeping and navigation.

He directs the weather and the storms, controlling where they go and who they affect and when. No storm strikes without His knowledge on what it is doing. He knows if a hurricane is due to strike a populated area, if a tornado is going to wipe out a city, or if an earthquake will bring a nation to its knees. He sends the rain and can call it off as He did with Ahab at Elijah's word. He also sends the rain on the just and the unjust. If a natural disaster strikes a major city, there are righteous and unrighteous people who are both affected.

Natural disasters are in part a result of the curse of sin. It is the groaning of the earth under the weight of the curse (Romans 8:22). The creation also reacts to God. When God came down in glory to Israel when He gave the Ten Commandments, there was lightning and thunder and the ground shook. When Jesus died on the cross, the sky went dark, the earth shook, and the temple veil was torn. Jesus spoke and the waves and winds died. He walked on the water and when He got onto the boat, the waves stopped.

The universe is not subject to the laws of science man has discovered and constantly tweaks. It is subject to the command of God to follow the pattern He sets until He gives another command. The winds, waves, mountains, valleys, stars, and planets all obey the command of God without question. Miracles are events that seem to defy the 'laws' of nature. God is the one who created this universe, and He does not subject Himself to the laws of how this universe operates. He operates as an outside source, able to intercede and direct the course of the weather for His purposes. He brought the storm which defeated the Spanish Armada in the battle with the English. He brought a horrific dust storm during a mission event in Juarez, Mexico so that the team could bring unused food to a needy orphanage. But He also allows nature to run its course. God is the overseer over the creation, which responds to His command.

Chapter 57: Patient

"But You, O Lord, are a God full of compassion, and gracious, Longsuffering and abundant in mercy and truth."
~Psalm 86:15

These are dark and evil times where wickedness has never been so prevalent. That which the previous generations would shame and hide from is now put in public for all to see. Mass shootings have become a norm in society. Sexual assaults and STDs have exploded. Violence, murders, rapes, theft, corruption, and all forms of evil are rampant. Many Christians are asking God, "How much more does it take for judgment to come?"

God is patient and long-suffering. While He does have every right to wipe man off the face of the earth, He longs for man to repent. He does not want to see any suffer under His wrath (2 Peter 3:9). He knows what His wrath is and what it would do to man. Many times, God will spare the many for the sake of a few. He offered that to Sodom with Abraham's intercession (Genesis 18). He also did that for Israel after the golden calf incident for Moses (Exodus 32). But in other cases, He struck one or two down so the many would not suffer the same fate. Nadab and Abihu in Leviticus 10 and Ananias and Sapphira in Acts 5 were struck down for offering profane fire and lying, respectively, and it spared everyone else. When Achan stole from Jericho, it cost Israel victory at Ai and because of him, his whole family had to be executed.

Was God patient with them? Not necessarily with those individuals, but He was patient with the whole group. He is also patient with many individuals. Paul was a wicked, violent, arrogant man before he met Christ. God was patient with him. But few illustrate God's patience with an individual more than Jacob. Jacob ran wild doing everything he could to get the blessings through cheating, deception, theft, or any other tactic. He did not finally get right with God until his fateful wrestling match with him in Genesis 32. While the Bible does not give his specific age at this moment, Joseph was already born and by calculating Joseph's ages in his time in Egypt with Jacob's arrival there, Jacob had to be at least 91 years old when he wrestled with God. God was patient with Jacob for 91 years. Moses was 80 when God brought him to the point where He could use him.

God is not only patient with individuals in their sinful state, but He is also patient with the process of purification and sanctification. He sticks with the process, no matter how long it takes, and waits through the stubbornness of man to deal with the issues.

However, God's patience does have limits. He will not strive with man forever as proven in Genesis 6. God's patience is not turning a blind eye. He will not allow sin to go unaccounted for forever. If a person or a people continually refuse to heed God's warnings, then His patience will one day run out and the judgment will come. It will be sudden, but it will not be without warning. It is a grave mistake to presume God's patience to be apathetic towards judgment. God is long-suffering, not willing for any to perish, but that is not grace to do whatever man wants to do. It is not to be taken for granted.

Chapter 58: Peace

"I will hear what God the Lord will speak,
For He will speak peace
To His people and to His saints;
But let them not turn back to folly."
~Psalm 85:8

Peace is often mistaken as the absence of war. War is often a result of a lack of peace. Peace is not a dream utopia either, though peace can include some of those features. Peace is when all is as it should be, when doubts are resolved, and wrongs have been made right. God is the God of peace, order, and structure. He makes all things happen in their proper place and time.

No person is at greater peace than when at the center of God's will and doing what they are supposed to be doing. A soldier facing the daily threat of battle in the Middle East is safer there in obeying God than staying home driving on the streets outside God's will. A person striving to arrive at a given destination, doing God's will, is going to arrive there. Hudson Taylor knew this. When his ship to China was disabled due to crashing at an island where cannibals were preparing a feast, Hudson suggested praying, knowing God had called him to China. The wind turned and sent the ship away. Paul also knew this. He was heading to Rome when after a shipwreck, he was bitten by a viper (Acts 28). He just shook it off and didn't think twice about it. Why? Because he had peace about his calling.

God offers peace even when bringing troubling news. Belshazzar experienced this in Daniel 5. When the writing on the wall came, he was so scared that he wanted an interpretation he knew would be true. Daniel came in and told him his time was up and his kingdom was to be overthrown. Belshazzar got bad news and yet because it was true, it gave him peace and he made Daniel the third-highest ruler in the kingdom.

God is the God of peace; Jesus is the Prince of Peace. In a world of chaos, He is the one who brings peace and order to it. Every area where there is no peace is an area run without God's direct control over it. There can be no peace without God's reign over that area. However, God does not want to give His people merely peace. He wants to give them Himself, because He is peace. Everything God does is about making peace or maintaining peace, all the while displaying all His other attributes.

The peace of God surpasses understanding (Philippians 4:7). It does not make sense how Paul could be stoned twice, whipped 5 times, imprisoned multiple times, shipwrecked twice, suffered numerous assassination attempts, and still have peace about it all. Reports of many Christians about to be executed show not fear but rejoicing. Ignatius is known for calling the Coliseum's lions his friends because they would escort him to Heaven. How is that possible? It is because they had the peace of God and knew the God of peace. Once peace is acquired, there is nothing that can stop a Christian.

Chapter 59: Pleasant

"Praise the Lord, for the Lord is good;
Sing praises to His name, for it is pleasant."
~Psalm 135:3

It feels good to be in the presence of God and to sing praises to His name. It is pleasant and pleasurable. Pleasure is not something to base one's salvation on, however, it is a God-given gift. Pleasure should not be ignored, however, it should not be foundational to one's decisions and worldview.

While pleasure is a God-given gift, it is also perhaps the most abused gift. The world offers pleasure as well, however, it only appeals to the flesh and it is always temporary, resulting in death. Every drug addict or alcoholic believed that the drug or the drink was pleasurable the first time they experienced it. However, after a while, the addicts found out what it really does and while enslaved to it, they utterly hate it. Every sinful temptation is about taking what God has provided and suggesting using it in the wrong way or in the wrong time. While it will be pleasurable for a moment, the pleasure will always fade.

The pleasure of God, however, never fades. Unlike the drug which requires more and stronger doses to give the same buzz, God offers deeper and purer pleasure with His being. God is pleasant, however, that pleasure is a byproduct of who He is, not a primary product. God never uses pleasure as a draw card, despite numerous evangelistic attempts at doing so. God does not promise a life of pleasure on this earth, but instead He promises persecution. The pleasure, while temporary here, will be permanent in the next life for those who endure to the end.

The world offers health, wealth, and prosperity, which also just so happens to be the same things Eve saw in the fruit of the Tree of the Knowledge of Good and Evil (Genesis 3:6), the three temptations Satan used on Jesus (Matthew 4), and the enemies of 1 John 2:16 as the lust of the flesh, the lust of the eyes, and the pride of life. Those are pleasurable for a season at best, however the sweet becomes bitter as it works its way through its course, and the result is death.

God offers pleasure as a result of seeking Him, and while pleasure is not promised here and now, God does not leave His people on this earth without it. The world does not understand how Christians can have such a good time with each other without alcohol, drugs, sex, etc. Christians find pleasure because we have Christ in common. Talking with other believers about Christ is fun to a Christian. If a person claims to be a Christian and talking about God is found to be boring, chances are that person never has been saved. How could anyone find the Savior of their soul to be boring unless their claimed faith is just a set of religious, mental statements to agree to, not about the Savior of the world?

God is not boring. He is pleasurable to those who have found life in Him. He is a stench of death to the perishing. God gives pleasure to those who seek Him and pursue Him with all their hearts. He never fails to go above and beyond what people of faith ask for.

Chapter 60: Preserver

"Oh, love the Lord, all you His saints!
For the Lord preserves the faithful,
And fully repays the proud person."
~Psalm 31:23

God preserves His people. He does not preserve them from experiencing trouble or pain, but He preserves them through trouble and pain. God has no desire to take His people around the storms, but rather to showcase His glory and His protection by taking them through the storms. Each person has their own storms to face, and they are often not the same. Some people have endured horrific childhoods due to sexual abuse, drunken parents, dealing with foster care, kidnappings, etc. Those who have not been through that have a difficult time ministering to those who have. But everyone has their own storms to go through, and God is able to preserve through such circumstances.

There are two types of testimonies: the rescue from the gutter and the preservation from the gutter. Most people think of only the former. "I used to be this, this, and that in my rebellion against God, but then God found me and now I am this, this, and that." The preservation from the gutter is for those who did not endure such circumstances but rather were protected from them. God needs both types of people. Those who came out of the gutter can readily go back into the gutter to save more like them, showing with their lives that one can get out. Those who were preserved from the gutter can support those going back in and give a demonstration of how to live outside the gutter.

Preservation from the gutter is purely on the grace of God, and few people truly realize how many times God has spared them from the gutter. The sinful nature is so wicked and so deceitful that unless the grace of God restrained it, it could make someone commit the most heinous crimes, making Hitler look like an angel in comparison. Romans 1 describes how those who repeatedly reject God's commands and refuse to recognize Him as who He says He is will be handed over to a reprobate mind. They will experience their sinful, lustful desires carried out in full fruition because that is what they wanted. The result will be death. Yet with many people, God has preserved them from such emptiness and despair.

God will often put His people through some trials and preserve them through others, to prepare them for their hour to showcase God's glory through them. David had 21 recorded assassination attempts on his life. Jesus had numerous times where the people tried to take Him. Paul should have died countless times during his ministry. John was thrown into a pot of boiling oil and came out unscathed. They could not be touched until God let them be touched. God preserved them though all sorts of trials. He will do the same with any who walk in faith with Him.

Chapter 61: Provider, Portion

"O Lord, You are the portion of my inheritance and my cup; You maintain my lot."
~Psalm 16:5

God is Jehovah Jireh, "My Provider." He provides for every need according to His riches and glory. He provides for all the birds and beasts of the field and the flowers. How much more does He want to take care of the needs of His people? Jesus said in Matthew 6:33 to seek first the Kingdom of God and His righteousness, and all these things will be added. What are these things? Food, shelter, clothing, all of man's physical needs, but often not all of the wants.

The Bible is full of accounts of God's provision for physical needs. In the wilderness, God gave Israel manna from heaven, water from rocks, and long-lasting clothing (they did not wear out). He fed Elijah with bread from ravens and water from a brook, then made a widow's oil jar never run out while the drought continued. He multiplied food for Jesus twice. But these accounts are not limited to just the Bible.

George Mueller did not like how many mission organizations raised their funds (by going from church to church asking for money) because it put their hope and trust in the churches and not in God. So, he wanted something not theoretical but tangible to prove that seeking God's provision by prayer alone works. He started an orphanage and never once told anyone other than his staff about their financial needs, even when asked. Not only did God provide for over 1000 orphans, He provided them with so much funding that Mueller could support foreign missionaries like Hudson

Taylor. Millions of dollars were funneled through Mueller. He didn't ask for a penny from anyone except God, and God provided.

God is the provider. His resources are limitless. He will provide what is needed, when it is needed, and according to how the recipient can handle it. He is never late, and He is rarely early. However, Satan had done a great job at getting people to seek the gift, not the Giver. He directly accused God of having to bribe people like Job to follow Him with provision and protection, so God said Satan could have at him but not take his life. Satan took everything away from Job, yet when it was over, God provided not only that which was stolen, but abundantly above what was stolen. God will not necessarily replace that which man loses by his own sin, however if the enemy steals from him, God will replace multiple times what was stolen if not more.

God is the source and supplier of all resources. Man can do nothing but manipulate what God has provided. From raw materials to money to time and even authorities, it is God who provided it. Jesus told Pilate that the governor had no authority except that which God had granted him. God is the provider for everything, but He allows man to choose how to use it. Use it wisely.

Chapter 62: Pure

"Your word is very pure;
Therefore Your servant loves it."
~Psalm 119:140

The fewer impurities in a precious metal, the purer the metal is. Yet the purest gold or silver cannot compare to the purity of God and His Word. Many people confuse innocence with purity. When Adam and Eve were created, they were innocent. They did not understand or truly know the weight of sin nor its effects. They understood God had said, "Do not eat of that tree," and they understood that death was the consequence, however they did not truly understand what sin would do to them. They were naked and unashamed of it. Why would they be ashamed? They were fully exposed with nothing to hide. But when they sinned, their nakedness became shameful. Their nakedness exposed their sin, and their innocence was gone.

Purity is similar to innocence but different. Innocence is a state of being and is often out of ignorance. Purity is a choice to stay untainted even when in a dark, corrupting environment. Jesus was able to eat and drink with tax collectors and sinners as well as attend parties where the guests all got drunk, and He stayed pure. Paul was able to walk through the marketplaces of Athens, seeing all the debauchery and idolatry, and not partake in the vileness. Lot was deemed the only righteous man in all of Sodom, where he grieved over the wickedness of the city. However, while Lot remained pure, his daughters did not escape untainted. Just because one can stay pure in a dark world, it is most unwise to enter that world unprepared and without a clear mission to rescue someone from it.

God's Word is pure, but it acts differently than man when it comes to entering darkness. Man can be affected and consumed by the darkness. God, however, is light, which cuts through the darkness. When God encounters sin, His purity and His holiness are so bright and strong that they clean the sin and destroy it. That is why God must separate Himself from sin. Sin is not God's "kryptonite." Yes, God cannot dwell in the presence of sin, but not because God is "allergic" to it. God is sin's kryptonite. If God were to be near sin, it would be destroyed just by His presence. God separates himself from man, so He does not kill him on the spot.

So little describes purity better than Jesus coming to live as a human being. He had never experienced sin. He lived in the presence of the Father and the Holy Spirit in perfect unity, and He laid it all down to live as a man. He knew no sin, but His body was still frail and mortal. He watched people sin all around Him, and it grieved Him to compassion. Even the air He breathed had been cursed from Adam's sin. Jesus frequently escaped into the mountains or the wilderness to pray and knowing this, it makes sense why. Yet, in all this, Jesus was exposed to all that sin and never once caved. He was pure, giving an example to all people. He will return for a pure, spotless Bride. Are we preparing for that day? Are we being made pure and into the image of Christ?

Chapter 63: Redeemer

"The Lord redeems the soul of His servants,
And none of those who trust in Him shall be condemned."
~Psalm 34:22

Redemption is one of the most central aspects to the Gospel. Jesus stooped down to wicked, sinful man, dying on the cross to pay the penalty for that sin on man's behalf, and thus redeemed those who repent and put their trust in Him. Redemption is an economic concept most known in terms of using coupons. When a customer has a coupon for a free item, he just needs to go to the cashier and hand the coupon over without having to pay for the item. The store does not lose any money because the coupon is a token of promise that the item has been purchased. However, the item cannot be acquired in this case unless the coupon is used. This is the same concept of redemption used to describe the Gospel.

When Adam and Eve sinned, they effectively sold themselves to Satan, to have him and sin rule over them instead of God. Paul makes it clear in Romans 6 that everyone will serve something or someone, namely either sin or Christ. Christ's work on the cross paid the penalty for sin and provided for the legal purchase of each person from the grip of sin. Because the price was paid, there is now a coupon available for each person.

The proper response to the Gospel is repentance and faith. One must confess (that is, say the same thing God says about it) sin as sin, repent from it (turn away from it and continue turning away from it), and put their faith and trust in Jesus to be the redeemer of their souls. Jesus takes the "coupon," which can be analogous to His blood, and purchases each person with His blood. In order for the coupon to work, it must be received. The response to the Gospel is the reception of the Gospel. That is different than acceptance as though it has to go through the person's approval for it to work. It has to be received where the person takes hold of what is offered and uses it. The cross made the "coupons" available, however, the coupons must still be used. This is why not all who claim to be Christian are Christian. The coupon of the blood of Christ must be used, and when it is used, when Jesus makes the purchase, that is when the Holy Spirit does His supernatural re-creating work, and the Christian is born again.

God longs to redeem every person because He does not want any to perish but all to come to repentance (2 Peter 3:9). The reason the coupon analogy does not fully work is because each person, the item in the analogy, must respond and receive it, whereas normal items don't have such a choice, but the redemption concept is still there. God is the great redeemer taking man from his sinful, wicked, muck-covered state, and washing him clean, purifying him into a spotless bride for Christ. The process is not complete and will not be complete until Jesus returns, but Jesus will not leave any project He starts unfinished. He will see it through to completion. He is the blessed Redeemer.

Chapter 64: Refuge, Shelter

"God is our refuge and strength,
A very present help in trouble.
Therefore we will not fear,
Even though the earth be removed,
And though the mountains be carried into the midst of the sea."
~Psalm 46:1-2

When Hurricane Andrew hit Florida in 1992, the mobile home parks were frequently shown to illustrate the devastating power of that storm. However, scattered throughout the destruction zone of the Category 5 Hurricane were the Palm Harbor mobile homes, the only brand which survived the storm. These homes were built with the intention of surviving hurricane winds and all other brands of mobile homes were wiped out.

Palm Harbor builds the strongest of mobiles homes, able to withstand Category 5 hurricanes. God, on the other hand, is a refuge who produces fearless confidence even if the earth be removed and mountains be cast into the sea. When God is the shelter and the place of refuge, it does not matter what is going on outside. This is no excuse to go in to hide and ignore everything else, however, what reason is there to fear if the shelter is guaranteed to hold?

People have faith in their shelters, or else they would not take shelter there. A police officer wearing a bullet proof vest does not fear a gun in the way he would if he was not wearing it. Different buildings are designed to handle certain disasters. Japanese homes wiped out in the 2011 earthquake were destroyed because they were not built to handle earthquakes.

They were built to handle typhoons. Because they could not handle quakes, they collapsed.

God is the refuge who withstands the entire world falling apart, so what reason is there to fear? The Christian can take refuge in Christ and then laugh at the storm battering him. Apart from Christ, the Christian would have every right to be terrified of such storms. God is the refuge, the shelter from the storm. If the political situation turns downright ugly, the Christian has no reason to fear because his shelter is in Christ. When persecution comes and the Christian is arrested and set to be executed, both he and his family can go through it with no fear because they constantly have their eyes on Christ. He is their refuge.

God is a shelter who never will fail no matter how bad the opposition gets. The more opposition a Christian faces in the shelter of God, the more confidence he will have in Christ, his shelter for facing all challenges. David escaped 21 recorded assassination attempts. He was protected because he made God his refuge. That does not mean he arrogantly dared Saul to come get him, but he had such confidence that it carried on to his Mighty Men who did extraordinary acts. Their shelter was their God, and it gave them utmost confidence. Why should we fear or worry? The King is on His throne. He's got our backs.

Chapter 65:
Rejected

"The stone which the builders rejected
Has become the chief cornerstone."
~Psalm 118:22

Jesus is the stone which the builders rejected and yet became the chief cornerstone. He came in a form no one ever imagined, born of a virgin girl in a stable, raised by a poor carpenter, and was not even good looking. He came into the spotlight as a servant, a teacher, and a miracle worker, but He never sought any attention and refused to take political action to overthrow Rome. Because Jesus did not fulfill the dreams of the Jews, He was rejected, despite perfectly fulfilling over 300 prophecies about who He would be, what He would do, how He would die, etc.

Jesus never sought any person's approval. In John 6, Jesus gave a very hard message right after feeding the 5,000 (men, not including women and children), and 20,000 people left Him. Jesus turned and asked His 12 disciples if they wanted to go, too. It is as if Jesus didn't care if people followed Him or not. He loved them, cared for them, and was compassionate over them; however, if they did not want the truth He offered, He was not going to chase them. He would have preached the same message even if no one listened to Him. He never once changed His message to make it "less offensive."

Following Jesus has a cost. It costs popularity, career paths, friendships, and ultimately one's own life. It is impossible to follow Jesus and be "cool" with this world. Those who try are hypocritical and double-minded. Jesus' requirement for following Him is death to self, the giving of everything a person is. It often is not much, but it must be all. Jesus does not settle for half-heartedness. In a world full of sinful, self-seeking masses, Jesus' message is hated to the utter extreme. Showing a sinful person the light of Jesus is not going to change them. It is just going to make them hate Him and His messengers even more. Why? Because sin and darkness hate light. The person must be exposed to the fact he is a sinner in desperate need of a Savior and recognize his plight before he'll come to the light.

Jesus knows what He offers, and He knows what happens without His gift. It grieves Him that people reject Him for no other reason than wanting to rule their own lives. The deception of sin is so powerful that it takes a supernatural intervention to break it, and that intervention only comes by means of prayer. He is constantly rejected by this world, and He will let this world do its thing bringing their own condemnation upon themselves. He is not waiting for man's approval as though they have to decide if He is worth their consideration. He is waiting for man to recognize his dire need and received what Jesus offers. But He will not wait forever. While this world rejects Jesus, Jesus also rejects the world. He was offered it if only He would worship Satan, but He would have none of it. Those who choose to stay associated with the world will go down with it, even if they claim the name of Jesus. Those who reject the world and abandon it to be with Christ, losing their own lives, will find their lives have been saved.

Chapter 66: Remembers Us

"Who remembered us in our lowly state,
For His mercy endures forever."
~Psalm 136:23

There are many Christians out there who wonder if God remembers about them or where He has them. Numerous people in the Bible wondered about that. Joseph was kidnapped by his brothers, sold into slavery, and falsely imprisoned, then when a chance to get out arrives, Pharaoh's butler forgot about Joseph for two years. But God did not forget about him, because when the time was right, He gave Pharaoh a dream and gave Joseph his time to shine.

Israel was enslaved by Egypt for centuries. Year after year, they cried out to God because of the brutality of the Egyptians. Then God remembered them and sent Moses to deliver them. Gideon had to thresh wheat in a winepress because Midian kept raiding Israel for its resources. When God showed up, Gideon asked where the God of the miraculous deliverance from Egypt was. Little did he know he was going to be part of the next miraculous deliverance.

God is never forgetful. He remembers where each person is in their life, no matter how dark the situation is. He has every hair on every head numbered. Some translations suggest every hair is named. He knows the stars, which are uncountable to us, by name. He knows when even a sparrow falls or when a rodent becomes roadkill. How much more so does He know where each and every person is?

Remembering has a connotation of "once forgotten, now recalled." The Biblical term is more accurately described as "bringing to the front of the mind." When God remembers something, it means He is making it His focal point. Memory in the brain is similar to that of a computer. There is short-term memory which is what is currently on the mind and long-term memory which is what has been learned but often takes a spark to bring to mind. Man has a temporal and a physical memory which means it has a limited ability and capacity.

God, however, is eternal and remembers everything. He keeps track of every detail going on all at the same time. He is working every aspect of every life together into one grand tapestry of history. Very often, He has to place someone in a dark pit somewhere to prepare them to make their move. Sometimes the pit is to train them. Sometimes it is to hide them. But in each case, God knows precisely where that person is, what that person's condition is, and what He is doing and going to do in that situation.

God has everything in the front of His mind. He remembers everything, except for one thing: the sins of those who have been born again and had their sin wiped clean by the blood of Jesus. He does not passively forget the sin. He purposefully does not hold that person accountable to that sin because it was dealt with on the cross. He will still bring it up on a rare occasion, but that occasion is explicitly for the purpose of correction and instruction, never for condemnation. He remembers every person and knows every situation, and His process is not yet finished. He will continue in that process until it is done.

Chapter 67:
Rest

"Arise, O Lord, to Your resting place,
You and the ark of Your strength."
~Psalm 132:8

It is a strange idea to think of God resting. He is infinite, eternal, and without limitation. How can a God with unlimited strength and energy get tired and need to rest? Yet in Genesis 2:1-3, God rested after six days of creating the universe and everything in it and setting the whole history of the universe into motion. Was God tired? Did He need to recharge himself? No. He was looking over His creation and with a great sigh of achievement; He enjoyed it. That is why He called the whole thing "very good" in Genesis 1:31. God did all His work and then He stopped and looked back to enjoy it as a work of art.

God's rest is not like the normal type of rest we humans picture. In Matthew 11:28-30, Jesus talks about all the weary and heavy-laden to come and get rest with Him because His burden is easy, and His yoke is light. What was He talking about? He was not talking about getting a night of beauty sleep and then going back to the heavy labor the next day. He was talking about the religious weight put upon the people by the Pharisees to keep not just the Law but all their little added laws as well.

Jesus offered a way to God that was not burdensome upon the people. How? The plan of salvation is not dependent upon the works of men to be achieved. It is acquired by the work of Jesus on the cross. A yoke is a pre-industrial revolution era plowing device where two oxen would pull the plow. It is what would connect the oxen together and to the plow. Often a young ox would be attached to a veteran ox, and while the young one would do some work, it was really the veteran who did the actual work.

The only 'catch' is that to receive this yoke and easy burden, one must shed the old yoke and discard the old burden and then submit to the new one. The Gospel cannot be accepted as though it goes through the person's approval. It must be received and embraced. The work is all on Christ, but for it to apply, it must be received. Once attached to the yoke there is work to do, but the work is being done by Christ through the Christian.

How is that rest? The Christian no longer has to work to achieve his standing with God. Even though he has a job to do, it is no longer toil nor tiring. The work he does is once again enjoyable and rewarding, whereas before it would be exhausting. Even after many years of labor were done, trying to work for your salvation would still never been enough, nor would there be any assurance that it would ever be achieved. In Christ, not only is all the work no longer being done by the person but by Christ, there is also assurance that the work by Christ will be completed. Then when each Christian's time is up, God will take them home when their work on earth is complete and they shall rest in His presence. Jesus is the rest for every believer. That is why the Sabbath is the only one of the Ten Commandments not reinforced in the New Testament, because its purpose was finished and fulfilled in Christ. Taking a day of rest is still important for the physical body, but the true rest is found in Christ.

Chapter 68: Restorer

"Restore us, O God of hosts;
Cause Your face to shine,
And we shall be saved!"
~Psalm 80:7

God is a restorer. He takes that which was broken, worn down, and good for nothing, and He fixes it. Many people think of a restoration in terms of old cars or an old building. They take an old, beat up car and they strip it of everything down to the bare frame. Then piece by piece, the restorer will replace the old parts with new parts, make sure all the parts work, and give it a fresh new paint job. In the end, the restored car looks exactly what the car should have looked like had it been brand new but with one minor difference: the restored car is more valuable than the car would have been brand new. The concept is the same for an old building.

Isaiah reinforces this concept in Isaiah 42:3. God will not toss out a broken reed nor a smoking flax. Reeds were very common in that area and kids would use them to make flutes. They are also very fragile and so numerous that if one broke, there would be no point in trying to fix it. Just get a new one. Flax lanterns required a constantly supply of oil to keep burning. If the oil ran out, the flax itself would start to burn with a truly horrendous stench that would force one to quench it or outright toss it as far away as possible. God will not toss aside a broken reed; He will restore it. He will not quench a smoking flax; He will trim it, refill it with oil, and put it back into use.

He does the same thing with man. Man was initially a flawless image or reflection of God. Man is not God but made to reflect the nature of God. But with sin, man became corrupt and the process of aging that leads to death began. The curse upon the earth prevented food from being able to completely restore all the energy which was expended to produce it. The Second Law of Thermodynamics reveals that there is no such thing as a machine that can just break even on the energy produced with the energy provided, let alone offer more than 100% efficiency.

But God is going to restore that function one day. Those who receive the free gift of God, who are washed clean in the blood of Jesus, and who are born again show a lifestyle of repentance and dependence upon Christ. They will be restored with glorified bodies that are not only what God intended them to look like initially but will be more valuable and more prized than when they would have been brand new. God is the ultimate restorer.

Chapter 69:
Rewarder

"The Lord rewarded me according to my righteousness;
According to the cleanness of my hands
He has recompensed me."
~Psalm 18:20

God is a faithful rewarder. He is not a briber; He is a rewarder. He does not say what the reward is because He does not want people doing their deeds for Him for the prize. He wants His people to follow Him out of their love for Him, not for what they get out of it. Satan accused God of bribing Job to follow Him. He said Job only worshipped God because God protected him, but if the protection was gone, he'd curse God to His face. God took Satan up on that bet and the rest is history.

Hebrews 11 is the famous chapter of the heroes of faith. Verse 6 in particular is of notice: God is a faithful rewarder of those who diligently seek Him. Proverbs 8:17 follows this train of thought of how God loves those who diligently seek Him. God does not and will not turn down any honest and diligent seeker. Any who seek after God with all their heart will find Him. In this case, the reward will not be riches or power but God Himself.

The Bible makes it clear that no one seeks after God, no not one (Romans 3:10-13). Each man is desperately wicked and depraved. In his own flesh, man will never seek after God. That is the sinful nature in a nutshell. The sinful nature is in direct defiance and enmity towards God. So how can any person honestly and diligently seek after Him? The answer is found in the Gospel of John: "No one can come to Me unless the Father who sent Me draws him" (John 6:44). The only way for any person to seek after God is for God to draw that person towards Himself. So, if God is drawing someone towards Him and that person follows, He will find God.

Galatians 6:7 warns that God will not be mocked, and a man will reap what he sows, both good and bad. Often each person is rewarded by what he plants. Though a common saying among churches in the farming communities is, "Man often sows wild oats [referencing sin] and then prays for a crop failure." Sometimes God allows for the crop failure and does not let the sin come back to haunt the person, but often He lets the sin do its thing. He also rewards those who sow good seed, however often that reward will not come in this life. Many times, the missionaries sow nothing but good seed and are met with opposition, hate, and in some cases death. But their reward will come in the new life.

The Bible is not clear what the reward is going to be. Some suggest it will be all the people brought into the Kingdom of God. It will not be in terms of wealth and money or political power because those things will be useless in heaven. What can very well be said is the reward is going to be bigger and better than anything anyone can image. And the best part of that reward is to be in the continual presence of God, removed from the presence of sin. That will be a glorious day.

Chapter 70: Righteous, Upright

"For the Lord is righteous,
He loves righteousness;
His countenance beholds the upright."
~Psalm 11:7

God is a righteous God. He can do no wrong. Everything He says and everything He does is righteous. God adheres to a perfect standard which is based on His character, and He is never lax with His standard. He always does the right thing at the right time. He gives mercy to those He will give mercy to and will administer justice when it needs to be delivered.

Abraham pleaded for God to the right thing and not punish the righteous with the wicked in Genesis 18. God was unable to find ten righteous people in Sodom and Gomorrah but in His righteousness, He pulled Lot out before the destruction came. Jonah did not want to preach to Nineveh because He knew God was both righteous and merciful, and if Nineveh repented, God might spare them. Jonah wanted Assyria (of which Nineveh was the capital) wiped out because of what they did to the kingdom of Israel and the other nations they conquered. God did what was right. He gave them the warning of the judgment and because they repented, even without an offer to do so, God spared them.

Job questioned how it was right for God to allow him to suffer the losses he suffered. He had done no sin that deserved such losses. He knew it, but his wife and three friends kept telling him that he must have sinned because in their understanding, bad things don't happen to good people. Job maintained his innocence and kept asking for God to explain why it was happening. That was when God showed up and in chapters 38-41, God asked Job a bunch of questions about how to manage the world and Job realized how little he knew. Job was a righteous man, God's champion, and yet he suffered seemingly on a whim of a bet between God and Satan. Was God wrong in putting Job through that? How right was it for God to send Jesus to the cross? God is not a fair God from our perspective, but He is a righteous God. So even while He will allow bad things to happen, He allows them for reasons we may or may not understand for some time.

A righteous God is going to see that justice is done both against the wicked and for the righteous. A righteous God must deal with sin. God cannot allow sin to go unpunished. But a righteous God also cannot allow the righteous to go unrewarded. He will and must do what is right, and He does that while allowing us the freedom to choose what we will do or not do. While He allows bad things to happen, He does not allow them to happen without His righteous judgment coming into play. The wicked will be judged, and the righteous will be recompensed. God is a righteous God and when all is said and done, He will make all things right.

Chapter 71: Right Hand

"Show Your marvelous lovingkindness by Your right hand,
O You who save those who trust in You
From those who rise up against them."
~Psalm 17:7

Jesus is at the right hand of the Father. The right hand is the symbol of strength and authority. Because most people are dominantly right-handed, the right hand is seen as the hand of strength and power. The left hand is often seen as the weak hand, and in many languages left means crooked or even unclean. Now this is no knock on the southpaws. The Bible praised a left-handed judge in Ehud, who was able to sneak a long dagger through security because he was left-handed (see Judges 3).

The reason the right hand is used so much is because it is the dominate hand for roughly 85% of the world's population. Had 85% of the population been predominately left-handed, the Bible would use the left hand as the symbol of strength, ability, and authority, and the right hand would be the hand for all the "weaker" and "dirtier" jobs.

Jesus is strength, the true source of power, and has all authority. He is the right hand of dominance, dexterity, and use. Apart from Jesus, man can do nothing productive. He is the vine; Christians are the branches. A branch separated from the vine is dead wood and produces nothing. He is the one who makes the sword in the hand move with speed, control, and precise accuracy. He is the one who makes the spoken word flow with life and power. He is the one through whom each person gets their food and sustenance.

If anyone tries to do anything apart from Christ, it will fail. Unless the Lord builds the house and guards it, it is built and guarded in vain (Psalm 127:1). One may be able to sustain it for a season, but eventually it is going to fade. If the house is built with wood, hay, and stubble, it may look good on the outside, but when fire comes, it will become nothing but ashes. But if it is built with gold, silver, and precious stones, objects which have already been formed and tested by fire, heat, and pressure, it will succeed. Only by building with Jesus as the source of strength, skill, and authority will there be success to last.

Jesus is more skilled, is more adept, carries more power, and wields more authority than any person can actually grasp, and yet He offers all of who He is to each of His children. All He asks in return is for each person to surrender all of who he is in a covenantal exchange. Jesus takes all the sin, the weaknesses, the frailty, and the failures, and each Christian in return receives all of Christ's power, His life, His strength, and His success. The reason Jesus was able to live the life He did as a man was because He was completely surrendered and yielded to the will of the Father. He claimed nothing of His own. Paul learned the same thing. He let Christ be his right hand and what a life he lived as a believer. When Christ is the right hand, there is nothing that will stop you in doing what He sets you out to do.

Chapter 72: Rock/Fortress

"The Lord is my rock and my fortress and my deliverer;
My God, my strength, in whom I will trust;
My shield and the horn of my salvation, my stronghold."
~Psalm 18:2

God is the rock, the fortress, a strong tower, and a hedge that protects all who put their trust in Him. A refuge is only as good as its strength, and its strength is determined by the structure of the refuge and the foundation it is built upon. If the foundation is weak, the refuge will also be weak. If the foundation is strong, the refuge will hold.

In Matthew 7:24-27, Jesus likens someone who not only listens to Him but also obeys Him as a wise man building on a rock, but those who do not obey Him as a foolish man who builds upon sand. In a desert such as the Middle East, when it rains, it pours, and it can carve mini canyons without too much problem through the desert sand. So when the house is built upon a large, solid rock, it is going to stand firm in the floods. If the house is built upon sand, while it is easy to mold and manipulate the foundation to one's own liking, when the storms comes, the flood will wash away the foundation and the house will collapse.

Missionary Bruce Olsen ran into trouble with trying to translate this passage for the Motilone tribe of Columbia as recorded in his biography, *Bruckko*. Building on a rock did not make sense to a Motilone because they had to dig into sand so the bamboo poles for their houses could grip something firm. He would not be able to translate this passage directly because the message would be lost. Instead, Olsen had to change the metaphor and would likely have translated this to: "He who listens to Jesus is as a wise man who digs deep into the sand and anchors his poles like a tree's roots" or something like that.

The challenge to building upon a rock is that it does not move nor alter its shape according to anyone's preference. However, the very fact that it does not move nor alter is also the very reason it can be trusted and depended upon. It is not going to move, which means when trouble comes, each person can know exactly where to go for shelter. It is not going to relocate and make people hunt it down. It also means it is solid and firm and will not collapse.

H.L. Hastings describes the Bible as an anvil which has worn out many hammers. The enemy will try everything in his power to demolish the anvil, however when the dust settles, the enemy's weapons are the ones worn out and the anvil still stands, unscathed. For 2000 years since the resurrection and the completion of the Bible, it has been under more intense scrutiny and vilification than any other event or book in all of history. Yet the Bible still stands with all opposition against it having been demonstrated to be false and failed. God is the Rock upon which all truth stands, and any who seek refuge with Him shall never be moved.

Chapter 73: Satisfies, Makes Full

"For He satisfies the longing soul,
And fills the hungry soul with goodness."
~Psalm 107:9

God satisfies every need for every person. He knows every need and know how to fill that need with what is going to do the job. God's provision does not always cater to taste buds or enjoyment but to what is needed. Many times, that which has a bitter or sour taste has a hidden function which helps the body. That's often why the medicine that works tends to not taste as good.

God gave Israel what they needed as they wandered through the wilderness. He made water come from a rock. He supernaturally gave them manna from heaven, and even their clothes never wore out for the 40 years of their journey. It was exactly what they needed: their daily bread. However, they began to remember the "benefits" of Egypt where they had a variety of foods. So, they demanded quail in Numbers 11. God was not pleased, not only because of their dissatisfaction but ultimately their rejection of Him being able to provide what they needed. So God gave them what they wanted: quail, so much of it that they would get sick of it and curse it. They complained because they did not receive the promises given them in the time they wanted. It was only in the next chapter that Israel arrived at Kadesh Barnea and looked into the Promised Land for the first time. After the spies returned as recorded in Numbers 13, the people refused to go in. They were not satisfied with God, not because God did not satisfy but because their greed, covetousness, and unbelief got in the way.

Proverbs 5 is a grave warning against the adulteress, who initially feels and tastes good but the end result is bitterness and death. The deception is that adultery, affairs, cheating on one's spouse, etc. may feel good because sexual activity is pleasurable. But if it is not done in God's way or God's timing, then the pleasure lasts only for a short season, and the result is a poison destroying far more than just the two people involved. But why do people cheat on their spouses? The answer is very simple: they find said spouse to be unsatisfying, so they seek to fulfill that desire in someone else. Why do they find them unsatisfying? Likely for the same reason Israel found God unsatisfactory. Not because the spouse was unsatisfying but because of a problem in that person looking elsewhere to get their desires fulfilled.

God satisfies every need, not ever desire, especially not desires of the sinful flesh. He told Paul in 2 Corinthians 12 that His grace was sufficient for him. Paul wanted a thorn removed because it was hindering him, yet it was there doing a job to keep him humble. God reminded Paul that he should be satisfied and content, even when things aren't where he'd like them to be. Those who trust in the Lord wholly will find that He satisfied every need to the point where they have no need to seek any other source to meet their need.

Chapter 74: Savior

"The Lord is my light and my salvation;
Whom shall I fear?
The Lord is the strength of my life;
Of whom shall I be afraid?"
~Psalm 27:1

Jesus is the Savior, the salvation for all mankind. It does not take astute observations to discover that people tend to get themselves into trouble quite easily, let alone having that trouble find them. There is a common story about a man who fled to the roof of his house during a flood and believed God would rescue him. A raft floated by, and he denied taking it because God would rescue him. A manned boat came by and offered to pick him up, and he denied the offer saying God would rescue him. Then a helicopter came and offered him space to get out, and he denied the offer saying God would rescue him. He drowned in the flood. When he got to heaven, he asked God why He didn't rescue him. God replied, "I tried three times and you would not listen."

God's plan of rescue comes in many ways, shapes, or forms. God is not going to provide a supernatural solution unless all of the natural solutions have been exhausted, and if a natural solution is available, God will likely use it first. In a financial crunch, God may not provide a sudden gift of cash to fill the need. He may grant a job through which that need might be met.

Israel's primary image of God being the Savior is rooted in the exodus. After being held in slavery for 400 years, God raised up Moses and supernaturally delivered Israel from

Egypt, the most powerful nation of the area. With the ten plagues and the famous crossing of the Red Sea, Egypt was annihilated. Israel had entered Egypt as merely one family, and they left Egypt as a nation. Whenever Israel called up God for a time of need, they always went back to this one thought: "The God who brought us out of Egypt."

God rescued Israel many times throughout the nation's history after this moment. Through periods of the judges and the kings, we see numerous battles and accounts where God came in for the rescue from empires, armies, plagues, famine, and more.

However, God is not merely interested in rescuing His people from their immediate circumstances but rather the bigger picture of rescuing us from sin, death, and self. Man's biggest problem is not really Satan or this world's system. Our biggest problem is self, and God desires to rescue mankind from self. But often man does not want to be rescued from self because he loves self too much. Yet, Jesus said self must die in order to be His disciple. Jesus is the Savior, the ONLY Savior. There is no other name by which man may be saved.

Chapter 75: Searches and Knows us

"O Lord, You have searched me and known me."
~Psalm 139:1

God knows every person better than they know themselves, and He knows every little detail about each person, both the good and the bad. His holiness and His purity often act as a searchlight, seeking any potential flaw or sin to deal with it. One of the most dangerous prayers a man can say is, "Lord, make me like Christ," because God will do that, and it will be at the complete and total expense of self. A very similar prayer that is just as dangerous is, "Lord, search me and try me. See if there be any wickedness in me." God's spotlight is penetrating, and it is impossible to hide from it.

God is going to expose sin one way or the other, and the best way to deal with it is to let God expose it in the prayer closet. If man tries to hide his sin, God may expose it publicly. David learned this this hard way. When he committed adultery with Bathsheba and tried to hide it by murdering one of his close friends (Uriah was one of his Mighty Men), God told him that because he tried to hide it, the same sin would be done in public (2 Samuel 11-12). That is precisely what Absalom did by taking in David's harem to a tent on the roof of the palace so all the people would see what was done (2 Samuel 17).

God's searchlight often works like editing a novel. During the first editing phase, the author will focus on looking for big plot holes or moving scenes to make the story flow better and get those straightened out. Then in the next phase the author will focus on smaller things, and this repeats several times.

Lastly, spelling and grammar take several run-throughs to catch the mistakes. All three phases are done together, but the general trend is to look for the big issues first, because if there is a major revision that needs to be addressed and re-written, the spelling and grammar phase will have to be redone again anyway. God's process of cleansing sin is similar.

He wants to get the big issues out of the way first, but He also knows to get down to the root of them. Sometimes He requires discipline in our lives so each person can focus on the fine tuning of areas in life. He may ask us to surrender TV, movies, and games so they are not distractions from the work He is seeking to do in each person's life. However, like an editor to an author, God is going to point out the problems, but each person must cooperate with God and trust Him that the corrections are for the best. When the author fights the editor, it rarely works out. God is the ultimate editor, and He will catch every mistake and knows precisely how to fix it.

When God is done cleaning, there no reason to fear His searchlight because it is only going to showcase all His work and not the sin He cleaned out. No one likes to show their home uncleaned to guests. They want clean homes to show around. God is the same way. Christ bought each Christian's body with His blood. He owns them and has the right to do with them as He pleases. He never lets one drop of blood go to waste, however, sin does a great job at hindering each person from being able to partake in God's mission. That is why He uses His spotlight to find it, then He'll dig down to the root and clean it out before replacing that sin with Himself. The end result is always better than the starting conditions. Let God search us and then let Him clean out all those areas that need cleaning.

Chapter 76: Shepherd

"The Lord is my shepherd;
I shall not want."
~Psalm 23:1

Psalm 23 is perhaps the most famous passage of Scripture behind John 3:16. "The Lord is my shepherd. I shall not want…" God is the Good Shepherd. This is often cited as a comfort, however it is not exactly a compliment for man. If God is the Shepherd, that means His people are sheep. Sheep are dumb animals. They are good at following each other, oblivious to where they are going. They are good at getting lost and in trouble. If they fall onto their backs, they are not capable of getting up on their own. A sheep is not able to live in the wild on its own, not merely for survival's sake, but also because its wool has to be constantly shaven.

God is the Good Shepherd. He knows how to take care of His sheep. When His sheep run into problems, it is because they have run away from the Shepherd. A shepherd usually has two tools: a staff and a rod. The crook in the staff has many uses, and one of them is to corral a sheep who wants to keep running.

The rod has two major purposes: for correcting and steering the sheep and for whacking wolves. Sheep, in their lack of brilliant minds, often need correction. Like with children, they need to be disciplined and trained to not do certain things. The rod can be used to tap them on the head or the back to encourage them along or to deter them from the wrong direction. The rod has another function in that it is strong enough to whack wolves. A sheep it utterly defenseless on his own, but when under the shadow of the shepherd carrying a weapon, the wolves don't have much of a chance to get the sheep. The Good Shepherd uses His rod correctly. He taps the sheep and whacks the wolves. Many people struggle with the balance and either tend to whack wolves too gently in fear of hitting a sheep, or they tend to whack sheep in the desire or need to smack the wolf. God knows how to balance the two approaches and never taps a wolf too gently nor whacks His own sheep.

Many sheep get devoured by wolves, and instead of turning to the Shepherd, they tend to turn to other sources. They may turn to alcohol or entertainment or something else to either subdue the pain or ignore it for a while. That does not get rid of the wolves. Sometimes sheep will go hire a wolf pack to go defeat another wolf pack, but then the sheep simply becomes a meal for someone else. Often those wolf packs are in cahoots together and they appear to 'fight' each other when they are working together. The correct response to a wolf attack is to go retreat to the voice of the shepherd. (Thanks to Eric Ludy in his sermon "Shepherding 101" for that image.) The shepherd can whip a wolf pack, but what makes the Good Shepherd unique is that He uses His sheep to fight the wolves with His strength. God knows His sheep have no power of their own, but if they tap into His power, He will beat the wolves in and through His sheep.

The Good Shepherd sometimes had to take His sheep through rough valleys and over mountains, but through it are lush green pastures. Let us follow our Shepherd. He knows how to tend His flock and how to care for them. He will never lead us astray nor abandon us to wolves.

Chapter 77: Shield

"The Lord is my rock and my fortress and my deliverer;
My God, my strength, in whom I will trust;
My shield and the horn of my salvation, my stronghold."
~Psalm 18:2

God is the shield for every believer. He is more than just a refuge for shelter in battle; He is the shield who goes before the army in battle. A shield is the first line of defense in combat. Soldiers wear armor should anything get through or around a shield, however, their desire is for the armor to not get hit. Shiny shields are shields that have never tasted battle and never been proven. The shields that are banged up are those that have seen war, and the soldier behind it is still alive.

God is not just a shield. He is the one who takes the hits for each believer. He is the great intercessor. An intercessor is one who stands between the person and an enemy to protect them. The purpose of an intercessor in battle is to find an ally who is knocked down, stand between the ally and the enemy to either take the hit or fight them off, and allow the ally to either get back up to fight again or retreat to the camp to rest, heal, and then rejoin the battle.

A shield doesn't work unless the soldier is behind it. A shield is meant to withstand the blow of a sword, arrow, bullet, or even a missile in battle so the soldier's personal armor does not have to. In ancient times, shields would often be made of wood covered in bronze. With modern police forces, a bullet proof vest often acts as the primary shield. In futuristic science fiction stories, shields are more like force fields. Shields only work for the soldier if the shield stands between the soldier and the weapon attacking them.

These shields, however, all have weaknesses. Wooden shields could burn, bronze shields could be bent out of shape, and all force fields could be turned off or have the generator destroyed. God, however, acts like a hand-held shield in close range combat and like a force-field against the powerful weapons, but He has no weakness. Psalm 18 describes God as a shield, but Psalm 91 shows how God acts as a shield in times of great danger, pestilence, war, and any other disaster. There is nothing that gets past God. The only things He lets through are what He purposefully lets through, and that purpose is to strengthen and build His people, or to present His people before the world as a testimony of who He is. But except for those moments, He is a shield, enabling a Christian to charge headlong through wave after wave of enemy fire and engage in battle unscathed. The shield of faith is one of the six pieces of the Armor of God in Ephesians 6, and absolutely nothing better illustrates how faith operates than a shield. A soldier must depend completely upon that shield to work to survive through battle. God is that Shield, and it is the responsibility of each Christian to hide behind that shield and charge into spiritual battle.

Chapter 78: Song

"The Lord is my strength and song,
And He has become my salvation."
~Psalm 118:4

There is a power in singing that many do not understand. God told Joshua to march around Jericho once for six days and seven times on the seventh day, and upon completion of the last lap to shout and sing. When Jehoshaphat faced three armies, he sent his army out to face them, however instead of making battle formations, he sent his singers and worshippers to lead. Why? Because God had promised victory without having to raise a sword.

Solomon established singers and worshippers to be at the Temple so that God would be praised 24/7. David's life was filled with singing. He sang while tending sheep, ministering to Saul, while on the run from Saul, when bringing the Ark of the Covenant to Jerusalem, and in many other times in his life. He is credited to 73 of the 150 psalms. David's son Solomon was no stranger to music either because he wrote 1005 songs (1 Kings 4:32), including the Song of Solomon.

Song and music have been an expression for joy, relief, grief, anger, and every kind of emotion. Music has the ability to skip the intellectual filters in the mind and go straight to the soul. This is also why it is absolutely critical to pay attention to what the songs are actually singing. A song may have an attractive beat, but each song has a spirit attached to it, and it could be good or bad. It is theorized that Satan used to be the minister of music before his great fall, and he is very good at using the music industry to poison the minds of people with images of sex, lust, drugs, murder, violence, hate, and all kinds of depravity.

But why should the devil have all the good music? God is the author of music. Satan can only corrupt it. Why let him take the lead in how it is used? Christian musicians should be leading the arts industries, not following distantly behind. There is no need to take the worldly music, slap Christian lyrics to it, and then rock and dance in the same Satanic and/or sexually driven manner that the world does. There is no need for 'cross-over' songs, songs which were written to God but work just as easily to anyone else. That is not worship. The Christian musician should be creative, not to win awards but to worship the King of Glory with the God-given talent he has been given, and not riding on what someone else has done. The way most people memorized Scripture so easily throughout the ages was by putting the words to music. But what about those who can't sing? Scripture says, "Make a joyful noise unto the Lord." It doesn't say it need to be "good."

The spontaneous praise of man to God Almighty has delivered men from many ills and defeated many foes. The song is not merely about God. God is the ultimate song. Music is able to lift the soul and press him on, but no song is able to do what God can do. God gives the song that needs to be sung. He is the subject of the song of worship. Paradise will be all about the worship of God, and it will not be boring. It will be exhilarating, soul-lifting, fun, and every other good adjective. Let our song be about God.

Chapter 79: Sovereign

"He rules by His power forever;
His eyes observe the nations;
Do not let the rebellious exalt themselves."
~Psalm 66:7

God is sovereign. He is not just the King over this world and the universe, but He has complete and full control over every little detail. God allows man to make his decisions, however not one decision made nor any consequences thereof are outside of His control. Many people cite Pharaoh during the Exodus or Nebuchadnezzar when he lost his mind for seven years (Daniel 4) as examples of how God can determine how a man can think. They will cite Jeremiah 18 when describing a potter and the clay, and they are correct to a point. God is in control.

However, God's control also uses man's choices. Little illustrates God's sovereignty more than in fulfilled prophecy, especially when the prophecy is fulfilled by the very enemies of God. When Judas betrayed Jesus, he received 30 pieces of silver. That silver was then returned to the Temple, cast down, picked up, and used to buy a potter's field in which Judas hung himself. This was predicted in Zechariah 11:12-15. Jesus, at the time Judas returned the money, was on trial if not already on the cross. How could He have orchestrated that?

It gets better. For Jesus to be the Messiah, he had to perfectly fulfill all 300+ prophecies made about Him plus the words He said. What does that mean? It means if Satan wanted to authentically disprove Jesus, it could be something as simple as trading Jesus for 20 gold coins, or 50 pieces of copper, anything except 30 pieces of silver. He messed up on that one. First Corinthians 2:8 tells us if the rulers (which includes Satan in his plotting) knew what they were doing, they never would have crucified Jesus.

God is sovereign. He can take the most wicked and evil plotters and still use them for His own glory and purposes, even as they rage against Him. What about those who seek after Him and follow Him? God is sovereign over their affairs too, and He will work all things, both good and bad, for their good (Romans 8:28). The Bible does not say things will turn out for the good of all. It says it will turn out for the good of those who love God and are called according to His purposes. When the wicked seem to have things under their control, God is still sovereign. He laughs at them, holding them in derision (Psalm 2:4). They can only play into His hands.

The world may be turning on its head, but none of it is outside God's hand. He allows the wicked to prosper but only in the same way a farmer allows his cattle to be fattened before the slaughter. God knows the end of the wicked and we have no need to fear them. God has such control over the affairs of men, angels, and demons that He can provide for His children and get the devil to pay for it out of his own pocket, all the while letting the devil think he is winning. God is in control. He is sovereign over all the affairs of man, and no amount of sin is going to remove Him from His position and rule.

Chapter 80: Strength, Power

"The Lord is my strength and my shield;
My heart trusted in Him, and I am helped;
Therefore my heart greatly rejoices,
And with my song I will praise Him.
The Lord is their strength,
And He is the saving refuge of His anointed."
~Psalm 28:7-8

God is the true source of strength and power in this world. He is mighty and able to do all things, even the physically impossible. Man can do nothing on his own strength. Even the very breath we breathe is enabled by God. While God gives each person natural talent, He gives supernatural power in and through His people who believe Him.

In Acts 1, Jesus states that when the Holy Spirit comes, the apostles will have power and will take His message to the ends of the earth. Those who are not just born again but have the indwelling of the Holy Spirit will have power to change this world. What kind of power? The power C.T. Studd had to go into interior Africa at 52 years old, with countless diseases from China and India when a perfectly healthy European man could die within three days, and he spent nearly 20 years transforming the Congolese jungle. The power Rees Howells had as he prayed through the battles of World War II, bringing miracle victory after miracle victory. The power David Wilkerson had in transforming the streets of New York when prior to going there, he knew nothing of street life. The power Amy Carmichael had to rescue 300 girls from temple prostitution in India.

None of these men and women had the strength of their own abilities to change the world, but the God they worshiped did. They would never have claimed to do those things themselves, but they only gave credit to God who strengthened them to do it. David slew Goliath not because he was skilled with a sling (he was, for the record) but because he trusted his God to give him the power to do the job. Nehemiah knew he lacked the strength or the endurance to build the walls of Jerusalem and yet he said, "The joy of the Lord is my strength" (Nehemiah 8:6).

The Seven Sons of Sceva (Acts 19:13-17) tried to call upon the power of Christ without having submitted to His authority. They called upon the name of Jesus whom Paul preached to cast out a demon and the demon replied, "I know Jesus and I know Paul, but who are you?" They lacked the power because they tried to ride on Paul's coattails claiming his power as their own. But they never had it. To carry God's power, one must first be under God's authority, not just in theory but in practice. It must be a lifestyle. The centurion in Matthew 8:5-13 understood this. He was under authority and had men under him. He understood that he only carried the authority of Rome by submitting to the authority of Rome. That's how Jesus operated and how Paul operated. They submitted themselves to the authority of God in action. That is why demons had to answer them, but not the seven sons of Sceva. God is the source of strength and power, and it can be accessed only in submission to Him.

Chapter 81: Sustainer, Upholder

"Though he fall, he shall not be utterly cast down;
For the Lord upholds him with His hand."
~Psalm 37:24

God is the sustainer of life. God is the one who gives the resolve to keep going and the oomph to get back up. When your tank hits empty and even the fumes are exhausted, God is able to keep you going. He has supernatural strength that He is able to impart upon His people. However, He often waits until the natural and physical strength are exhausted before administering it.

Athletes understand this notion to some degree. There is a physical and mental wall during an event where the body feels wiped out, but if the athlete is able to push past that wall, they can get a second wind. For the marathon runner, the wall hits a few miles in, but once past the wall they can finish all 26 miles. God works in a similar way. He lets all the physical energy get consumed so the believer is completely dependent upon Christ, and as long as the believer does not quit, then the barrier is broken and there is new strength. Every missionary who has learned how to depend upon Christ's strength knows this secret. Prayer follows the same pattern. It takes God to break through the barrier and then the throne of grace will be reached.

God takes the physically weak, the intellectually humble, the financially poor, and those who have no resources of their own to showcase His strength in and through them. He sustains them beyond what any natural means can produce.

Nehemiah was running out of strength because of not just the intensity of building the wall of Jerusalem but constantly receiving threats and taunts from Sanballot, Tobiah, and Geshem. Those three came at Nehemiah in nine different ways, and at one point Nehemiah cried to the Lord, "Give me strength." He was beyond exhaustion and yet he maintained his strength.

Moses did not even begin his journey to deliver Israel from Egypt until he was 80 years old. He walked with Israel for 40 years, guiding them right up to the Promised Land, and his strength never waned. God sustained his strength well beyond his normal years. Time and time again, those who trusted in the Lord found strength and supply well past their natural means. The widow's oil and flour never ran out when taking care of Elijah. Another widow's oil never ran out until she ran out of jars to put it in at Elisha's word. When Jesus had just spent a full day of ministry, He sent the disciples across the lake to rest, and the crowd beat them to the other side. While there, Jesus, knowing they were fully exhausted, told them to feed them, and 5000 men were fed. God was their sustainer.

God is the sustainer and upholder of His people. The tasks He gives are impossible in natural strength, however He is the one who provides what is necessary to get the job done. If the fuel runs out, God will provide in some way, shape, or form. He will provide the fuel when it is needed, or He will not let the fuel run out. He has done that in many different ways not just in Scripture. He will sustain His people who rely upon Him for their resources.

Chapter 82: Teacher, Instructor

"Good and upright is the Lord;
Therefore He teaches sinners in the way.
The humble He guides in justice,
And the humble He teaches His way."
~Psalm 25:8-9

Many people complain about how life does not come with an instruction manual. In reality, it does come with one; many just don't like it. The instruction manual is the Bible, and God is the teacher, teaching from the manual. The Bible gives the instructions necessary for every aspect of life. The Bible does not teach on how to manage video games or coal mining, however it does teach on how to handle entertainment and how to handle jobs and management.

This life can be likened to classroom education. The purpose of education is to prepare the student for life or the job he will take on. It is a short season intended to prepare for a lifetime of living. Likewise, this life on earth is a short season intended to prepare for eternity. It is not a perfect analogy, but the general concept is there. Jesus spoke repeatedly about how what happens in this life will be rewarded in the next. The servant of the least of these will be praised as the greatest in heaven.

Education has a test system, however that test system is nothing more than, "Can the student demonstrate to have mastered the material given?" Many students come through high school and college, can have straight-A's, and can come out not knowing much because all they learned was enough material to pass a test and two weeks later lost it all. God's tests are not like the educational system. It is not based on a scale of 0-100, nor are results given a statistical value like a letter grade. It is not based on Biblical knowledge (though having sound doctrine is important). It is not based on works or humanitarian aid or tithing. It is rather based on the heart and its condition. God's tests are based on whether the student trusts and believes Him or not.

David did not pass the moral exams. He committed adultery and murder. But no one else had a heart that yearned after God like his did. Saul tried to pass the sacrificial exams, but Samuel told him that obedience was more important than sacrifice (1 Samuel 15:22). The Pharisees passed the exams about the law, however they failed to pass the heart test. The publican who prayed a humble prayer failed all the moral exams and yet he passed the heart test, not because of anything he did but because he recognized his sin as sin. The publican's heart was ready to receive the Gospel and the work of Christ on that cross.

The Bible is the instruction manual. In Romans 7, Paul even described the Law as a schoolmaster. God is the teacher. He teaches the correct way. He identifies the wrong way. He shows how to get off the wrong path and how to get back onto the right path. He is a Good Teacher.

Chapter 83: Trustworthy, Sure

"The works of His hands are verity and justice;
All His precepts are sure."
~Psalm 111:7

God is trustworthy and dependable. Everything God says that He will do, He will do. If He wants it to be done, it will be done. Any person who puts his trust in God can be assured that God will do what He says. However, there are two fallacies that are easy to fall for regarding God's dependability.

The first fallacy is presumption. When Jesus was tempted in the wilderness, one of the temptations was to presume God would come through on a promise He made. Satan quoted Psalm 91 that Jesus would be delivered by throwing Himself down from the Temple and angels would catch Him. Jesus responded with, "You shall not put the Lord your God to the test." God did carry out Psalm 91 throughout Jesus' life, frequently delivering Him from trouble and attempted executions before His time. However, Jesus did not presume God would take action and try to force His hand.

The second fallacy is assuming God is going to answer a prayer given without hearing an answer from Him. There is a great cry about the problem of evil and when bad things happen, what is God doing about it? A child prays for his mother to be healed from cancer and she dies. A girl begs God every night that her father would not come into her room to molest her but it happens. How can God be trusted when He can't seem to take care of these issues? With complete respect to the pain of such cases, what did God say about the situation? Did He say He would heal this person or stop that evil in the timing asked?

Jesus did not promise a life of peace and prosperity. He promised a life of difficulty and persecution. The peace and prosperity are promised for the next life, not this life now. It grieves God when the sick die and children are hurt, but that does not mean He is not doing anything about it, nor that He won't do anything about it. Every child molester will receive just punishment sooner or later. God has promised that. No one knows why God allows cancer to take a loved one, but God has the full story in sight, and He allows everything to take place for a reason. He is sovereign and He will vindicate the righteous and the innocent.

When God says He will do something, He will do it. If God did not say He would do it, He is under no obligation to do it. When people pray according to the pattern God set, He will answer those prayers. In that pattern, God will answer the prayers He initiates. When God sets His heart upon someone, He will give that person His heart and His mind over a given situation to pray in that manner. Then God expects that person to keep praying until the answer has been given. God is faithful and trustworthy, and He will deliver on every prayer He initiates. Even when man is faithless, He is faithful. He will never go back on His Word, and every person can stand with boldness and proclaim what He said He would do will be done, and then act in faith, living as though the promise has and will be fulfilled. God is trustworthy and dependable.

Chapter 84: Truth

"For the word of the Lord is right,
And all His work is done in truth."
~Psalm 33:4

God is the Truth. He is the standard upon which all standards must be compared. The Bible is known as the "canon," also known as a rod. One of the ways the word 'rod' is used is as a measuring rod. In science, time is measured in seconds, length in inches and feet, weight in pounds, temperature in degrees Fahrenheit, etc. In France, there is a museum where the formal definitions of the metric units are held. All meter sticks, weigh scales, clocks, thermometers, electric meters, etc. are calibrated to match the standard at this museum. If there is any discrepancy, the measuring device is considered to be faulty. But if there is a perfect match without a single flaw, the device can be considered valid.

The same is true with God and His Word. He is the standard upon which all other standards are to be judged and measured. There are many standards we use: social standards, scientific standards, church standards, family standards, ethical standards, etc. There is not necessarily anything wrong with having these, however there is one standard that rises above them all: God's standard. Any standard that desires to compare with the Bible must prove to come from God, be in perfect unison with that which God has already authorized, produce the same fruit, and be publicly sealed as having that same authority at the time it is written. Those are the tests used to determine which books of the Bible were to be included in the canon of Scripture. Any other standard can be okay to use for certain circumstances, but it is not divine nor supreme.

Because God is the truth, He cannot lie (Numbers 19:24). That also means He cannot violate a single one of His attributes, even in favor of another attribute. Everything He says and does is truth, even if it makes us feel bad. In Daniel 5, Belshazzar wanted the truth when the hand wrote on the wall. Daniel told him the news that his kingdom would be overthrown and because he spoke the truth, the king granted Daniel the #3 position in the kingdom. In 1 Kings 22, Ahab and Jehoshaphat weighed in to see if God wanted them to go to war, and 400 prophets all said they would win. Jehoshaphat knew better and asked if there was any real man of God left. There was one, Micaiah, who told the truth on how God allowed a lying spirit to convince Ahab to go to war. Even with this, Ahab was still persuaded to go leading to his death. The truth will often hurt, but there can be no peace without it.

God is the truth. He is the standard. He is the one everything must compare to. He is a standard man never can never match. Yet there was one who could: Jesus Christ. He perfectly met God's standard because He is God. He perfectly aligned to the measuring rod, therefore He was able to do the impossible and be the Savior for all. In His perfect match to Scripture, that means He, too, has the same authority. Everything He says and does is as though Scripture said it. God is the Truth, the standard of all standards.

Chapter 85: Vindicator

"Vindicate me, O Lord,
For I have walked in my integrity.
I have also trusted in the Lord;
I shall not slip."
~Psalm 26:1

God is the vindicator of the righteous. There is great wickedness in this world and many crimes committed against the innocent and the righteous. God is going to see that justice is done. Many argue, "Why couldn't God have simply prevented it from happening?" The answer is that while God is sovereign and still all-powerful, He chooses to allow man to make his choices and do what he wants to do. But He never allows those choices to be without consequences. If God were to stop every child rapist before they do their heinous crime, by His standards of righteousness, He would also have to stop every person who simply does not believe God's standards, including the doubter from even asking that question. This doubter should instead ask how a good and righteous God could know what he did the night before and not kill him in his sleep.

The people who make these objections do not view God's standards of morality as being *the* standard but their own. They are quick to judge those whom they deem more wicked than they are, but they are also quick to excuse themselves for their own sins. God is a God of justice, and every sin both great and small will be met with justice in one way or another. The child rapist will receive his due just as the little white liar will. That being said, the victim of the child rapist will have justice done on his or her behalf because God is a vindicator of the righteous.

It is God's job to administer justice, and He will do it in His pure and perfect way. He desires to give mercy, but even in that mercy, it will not be without consequences. Each man will reap what he sows, and when one sows wild oats, he should not count on a crop failure to save his hide. Repentance from sins does not necessarily stop the consequences from taking place. David learned that the hard way with his adultery with Bathsheba and murder of Uriah. He repented immediately when Nathan confronted him (2 Samuel 12, Psalm 51), however Absalom would become the fulfillment of all the evil David did when he murdered his own brother (2 Samuel 13), and raped David's harem (2 Samuel 17). Uriah's death was vindicated.

The righteous may not see the vindication of the sins committed against them in their lifetime. It may be years down the road. God thinks in terms of generations, not just individuals. When Amalek attacked Moses in Exodus 17, God would not deliver the consequences of such actions until 500 years later when He told Saul to wipe them out in 1 Samuel 15. Why did He wait? God was waiting for them to repent, but they did not.

There is no need for revenge when a wrong is done. God is going to take vengeance when the time is right and in the right way. The righteous and the innocent will be vindicated, and their cause will have justice executed for them. It is God who will do it.

Chapter 86: Wash, Cleanse, Purge

"Purge me with hyssop, and I shall be clean;
Wash me, and I shall be whiter than snow."
~Psalm 51:7

Psalm 51 is the famous song of David's repentance from his adultery with Bathsheba and the murder of her husband, Uriah, to cover it up. Here David truly recognized and realized how wicked and sinful his heart was. He realized was born in sin, his sin was an ever-present blight upon him, and he knew the only solution was not good works to cover it but to get washed clean, to have his sin purged from his very being.

God offers each person a clean slate, a chance to start over. The debt of sin is unpayable except with blood. To go against God's standards even once, even for a "small thing," requires the taking of life. Yet, God offers a clean slate to the wicked criminal. How is that possible? The cross is considered a scandal for a reason, because God justifies the wicked and let an innocent person die in their place. The reason it works is because Christ was willing, not because God is a corrupt judge.

The blood of animals could only cover for sin temporarily. That is why it had to be done on a daily and yearly basis. The blood of Christ did much more than cover sin; it cleaned and purged it. The blood of Christ is like a soap agent against grease and oil. It binds with the sin, pulls it out, and washes it away. Isaiah 64:6 describes man's own righteousness as filthy rags. The concept is alike to menstrual rags or even leprous rags. Clothes that were stained by an inward problem now exposed themselves on the outside. Man's own righteousness can only cover the disease for a short season before becoming corrupted themselves. Christ's blood, however, is able to get to the core of the issue and cleanse it.

The life of a Christian should be a perpetual process of cleansing and purging of sin. Often it takes a while to get the job done, but that is what sanctification is all about. It is about removing sin and separating that area once infected by the world and by sin to be holy and pure for God. God frequently works one area at time in the same way He had Israel conquer the Promised Land one area at a time. The reason it had to be a gradual process was because Israel was not yet in position to possess the whole thing without wild animals or other nations coming in to take over. The same concept applies here. God washes one area at a time so it can be mastered and conquered for Him, rather than doing it all at once lest an enemy come in and reconquer.

No parent loves to clean the mess of a baby's diaper. Yet, God takes great pleasure is wiping our messes clean and disposing of them. A parent knows the baby is much happier without having to deal with that mess and having a clean bottom, and the parent is happier, too, without that smell lingering. God is the same way. He knows the mess is there and He wants to clean it so the stench is no longer around. The blood of Christ is the cleansing agent, and when it is applied, the sin is gone and disposed of. The end result is a pure and spotless Bride for Christ.

Chapter 87: Warrior, Commander

"You are my King, O God;
Command victories for Jacob."
~Psalm 44:4

God is a Warrior and our Commander. He is not just an instructor for war, He is Himself both warrior and commander. The greatest generals and leaders were not merely ones who commanded from the backfield but were there standing in the front line with their allies. William Wallace commanded the armies of Scotland not as a noble watching from his horse in the back but in leading the charge himself. King David was also such a leader. In fact, when one of the giants slain by Abishai (2 Samuel 21:15-18) tried to kill David, Abishai told David to stay out of the battle lest he be killed. Prior to that, David was right there fighting with everyone else.

God is the same way. He is not a distant commander but an active, personal, lead-by-example commander. God will never send a single one of his soldiers into a battle He will not fight Himself as one of them. Some of God's battle plans will seem utterly ridiculous. He told Gideon to shrink his army from 32,000 to 300. He had Joshua march around Jericho. He told Jehoshaphat to prepare for battle but would not need to lift a single sword.

God also uses weak people to beat the strong. Saul was Israel's giant, head and shoulders above everyone else. He was a strong man. Yet when Goliath came calling, Saul cowered as did all his soldiers. But 40 days later, a lad not even of fighting age showed up as a messenger and delivery boy, heard the giant, and slew him. David was not trained for battle, but he knew who the real fighter in the battle was: his God. David would become a great warrior winning battle after battle, leading by example. The only time he did not lead for war got him into the trouble with Bathsheba in 2 Samuel 11. When men do not go to war when they are supposed to, sin lies at their door and takes them down.

God is a warrior and a commander. While there is great evil going on today, the day is coming when Christ will return on a white horse, carrying a rod of iron and with a sword coming from His mouth. He will slaughter the wicked who repeatedly despise His name and rail against Him. He will fight for the righteous, and His army will be at his side, not to fight but to watch Him win the ultimate victory in the grand finale. He fights for His people, and those who do their battles on their knees get to participate and watch Him work.

Chapter 88: Wise, Wisdom

"To Him who by wisdom made the heavens,
For His mercy endures forever."
~Psalm 136:5

God is wise. He is not just all-knowing; He is wisdom. Having knowledge is one thing; using it correctly is another. God's wisdom is exceedingly above and beyond the wisest wisdom that men have. First Corinthians 1 describes how the foolish things of God are still wiser than the wisest of men. When the most educated men rise up and try to outsmart God, He will take something they consider to be foolish and knock them down a few notches.

Isaiah 55:8-9 describes how God's thoughts are higher than man's thoughts and His ways are higher than man's ways. Many people cite that passage to suggest that no one can know God or what He thinks. That is rubbish. Yes, God's ways and methods are far greater than anything man can offer, however God has revealed Himself to man so that he can know Him intimately. The Christian has access to the mind of Christ (1 Corinthians 2:16). It is very possible to know and understand how God thinks and what He plans and His wisdom - as much as God desires to reveal to us. It is not by education but by studying Him and His Word. Those who read the Bible learn how God acts with His people, how His mind works, His methods, and His preferences. The Bible does not give every detail, but it certainly does not leave man clueless about God.

Solomon was considered the wisest person to live because he asked for wisdom on how to lead. People from all over the world, including the Queen of Sheba, came to test him to find out how smart this man was, and he was able to give an answer to everything she asked. The only area where Solomon failed to exercise his wisdom was in his choice of brides because they led to his downfall. Yet Christ was wiser than even Solomon. The Pharisees tried all kinds of ways to trick Jesus with loaded questions, and He never took the bait in a single instance.

With wisdom, God created the heavens and the earth. He did not leave anything to random chance or gradual "evolving." With wisdom, God maintains the universe, holding every atom in place. With wisdom, God governs over the affairs of man, setting up rulers, putting them down, and even looking into the small details such as locating car keys that seemed to go missing. With wisdom, God directs people to move from place to place, setting up connections as necessary, and positioning them to do the job He desires. With wisdom, God grants the knowledge and discernment to some, and He pulls it from others, so outcomes turn out as He desires. Adolf Hitler was a military genius and yet multiple times during the rescue at Dunkirk, the D-Day invasion, and other battles, he made some boneheaded mistakes. Prayer warriors like Rees Howells were actually praying for him to make mistakes so the allies could win and put an end to Hitler's evil. It was God who grants the military genius his wisdom, and He can also remove it.

God is the source of wisdom, and He urges men to seek wisdom above riches, above power, above reputations, above even education, because when wisdom is sought, so is God. He will grant wisdom to all who seek Him.

Chapter 89: Wrath

"Then He shall speak to them in His wrath,
And distress them in His deep displeasure."
~*Psalm 2:5*

One aspect of God that many skeptics hate and dread is that God is a God of wrath. He hates sin with perfect and pure hatred, and it is only His mercy that holds it back. God knows the strength and power of His wrath against sin and what it will do to man should it be unleashed. A common image given about God is this: with one hand He holds His wrath back, keeping it from striking at sinful man, and with His other hand, He beckons man to come to Him for protection from that wrath. However, that wrath will not be restrained forever. The day will come when both hands drop.

Sometimes, God unleashes his wrath upon a single person to save the whole group and get them back in order. He did that with Uzzah in 2 Samuel 6. David carried the Ark of the Covenant on a cart, instead of on poles on the shoulders of Levites as commanded. When the cart began to tumble, Uzzah, in his pure intentions, touched the ark and God killed him on the spot. It wasn't his motive that got him killed; it was sinful man touching the holiness of God. In Acts 5, Ananias and Sapphira lied about how much money they gave to God. God killed them to remind the church to take Him seriously.

Other times, God wipes out a nation or a city because of sin. He destroyed Sodom and Gomorrah because of their exceeding violence and sexual perversion. He also drove out the inhabitants of Canaan during the conquest, not because of

Israel's status, but because they were committing the very sins listed in Leviticus 18. Nineveh's violence drew God's judgment and only their repentance at Jonah's preaching spared them.

God also punishes nations for a single man's sin. Joshua lost a battle at the tiny town of Ai because one man, Achan, stole some plunder from Jericho. God had him and his family executed. In the wilderness when Israel began taking other wives in defiance of God's order otherwise, God sent a plague against them, and it was Phineas who took a spear and killed an Israelite and his Midianite wife, in zeal for the Lord, which staved off his wrath. In Numbers 14, God told Moses that Israel had tested Him 10 times, provoking Him to wrath to wipe out the whole congregation. God hates sin.

There is a teaching that God's wrath was satisfied at the cross. That is only true for those who are born again, not for the unbeliever. It is God's righteousness and perfect standards that were satisfied at the cross. Sin was defeated there, but it is obviously still present. Revelation 16 describes how God's wrath is building in bowls soon to be poured out. God's wrath against sin will never cease, even after the end of this world because those who will suffer in hell are going to experience His wrath for eternity. God hates sin. Proverbs 8:13 states that the fear of the Lord is to hate evil. It is impossible to love God and love evil. By its very definition, sin is willful and defiant rebellion and treachery against God. God hates sin, yet He offers mercy for those who will receive it. But He does not offer that mercy forever. The day will come when his wrath will be unleashed. Those who do not believe in Christ will bear its full force.

Chapter 90:
Zeal

"Because zeal for Your house has eaten me up,
And the reproaches of those who reproach You have fallen on me."
~Psalm 69:9

God is a zealous God. He has pure passion for His name's sake and for His Kingdom. It was God's zeal that motivated Jesus to drive out the sellers and buyers at the temple. It was zeal that initially drove Saul to persecute the Christians and zeal that drove him to preach the Gospel to all peoples. David was known as a man after God's heart. He frequently messed up and did things wrong, but so few had a heart where with everything he had, he sought after the Lord. He was zealous for the Lord.

God does everything He does with passion. He never does anything half-heartedly. He never gives only partial effort. He gives everything to what He does. He is patient and takes the time to get done what needs to get done when it needs to get done, and He always goes all the way. When He issues mercy, He doesn't just give a little mercy; He gives all mercy. When He loves, He loves fully, purely, and passionately. When He hates, He hates perfectly and passionately. When He created, He made it all "very good," and not half-done so "natural causes" can take over. When He blesses, He goes exceedingly above and beyond what man can imagine. When He curses, He lets it work its full purpose. When He saves, He saves completely. In everything God does, He does it to the fullest measure.

God is zealous for His people. That is why He gets jealous over them. He does not want anyone turning to other sources of life, joy, fulfillment, provision, or anything else because He is zealous that they seek Him, the only one who can actually satisfy those needs. The world always has an answer to man's needs, but it never fully gets the job done. Only God can do it. God is zealous that we have our needs fully met, and He is the only one who can do it. That is part of why He issues no other gods and no idols as the first and second commandments. God has to be first, not because His pride is at stake, because He is the only one deserving to be first.

God is zealous for his Kingdom. He is the Creator and therefore the rightful king over everything. He will not tolerate man ruling over anything God did not give Him the right to rule. Man was given dominion over the Creation, but he was not given the right to rule his own life his own way. Man has always needed God's input, direction, and rule. Adam's sin was a coup in attempt to dethrone God from His rightful place and He is zealous in everything including His rule. Man's attempted coup never pulled God off the throne, but it put him at war with a zealous God who loves wholly and hates rebellion wholly.

God is a zealous God. He goes all the way. He never leaves anything behind. He never quits a job He starts. He never leaves a project until it is completely done and done right. He never tires at going all out. The best part is that His zeal is contagious. Those who seek after God's heart receive His heart and His zeal. Paul got it. David got it. Nehemiah got it. Every born-again Christian can get it. The zeal of the Lord is a great thing to have.

About the Author

C. A. Wolcott is a rising speaker and author out of El Paso, Texas. His greatest passion is to share the truth of the Gospel. He was raised on the mission field helping his parents as they served with International Family Missions for 22 years. He is active in his church and teaches a Bible study group every week. He teaches physics at a local high school. One of his favorite hobbies is the sport of fencing where he competes and coaches at a local club.

He joined Worldview Warriors in January 2014 and is constantly looking for ways to share his faith. He is a graduate of the 11th "Cadre" program from the Creation Truth Foundation where he was commissioned to teach about the importance of having a Biblical worldview and to defend the faith with apologetics. With that, he has spoken at several conferences, church events, and Christian school assemblies on a variety of topics. When he is not speaking or teaching, he is an author. Check out his author page at cawolcott.com for more details.

Equipping Students to Impact This Generation
For Jesus Christ

www.WorldviewWarriors.org

Worldview Warriors
P.O. Box 681
Findlay, OH 45839

info@worldviewwarriors.org
(419) 835-2777

We provide free weekly resources available to use in personal study, small groups, Sunday school classes, sermons, etc.

Contact us to book Charlie Wolcott or one of our other speakers for interviews or your next event!

Find us on Facebook
www.Facebook.com/WorldviewWarriors

DONOTKEEPSILENT

Speaking out the name of Jesus Christ in action and in word

DO NOT KEEP SILENT

This is the talk radio show and podcast for the ministry of Worldview Warriors. Tune in to hear great music and Biblically based teaching for those wanting to expand the Kingdom of God.

90.1 FM - WXML in Upper Sandusky, OH area
Sunday evenings from 7pm - 9pm

You can find all of our audio programming at
www.worldviewwarriors.org/programming/

DoNotKeepSilent.com

Facebook.com/DoNotKeepSilent

Other Books by C.A. Wolcott

Biblical Foundations: Basic Christianity and the Reliability of Scripture
By C.A. Wolcott

Ten Reasons to Believe the Bible
By C.A. Wolcott

www.ingramcontent.com/pod-product-compliance
Ingram Content Group UK Ltd.
Pitfield, Milton Keynes, MK11 3LW, UK
UKHW021909190726
13853UKWH00002B/586

9 798544 72164